Millwood
Hospital

# MY TESTIMONY

# MY TESTIMONY

## HOW GOD USED THE PAIN OF MY DATING RELATIONSHIP TO GET MY ATTENTION AND HAD ME RETURN TO HIM

## ARQUILA A. TODD

**Outskirts Press, Inc.**
**Denver, Colorado**

My Testimony
How God Used the Pain of My Dating Relationship to Get My Attention and Had Me Return to Him

All Scripture quotations, unless otherwise noted, are taken from the HOLY BIBLE: NEW INTERNATIONAL VERSION (Study Bible Edition). Copyright © 1973, 1978, 1984, by International Bible Society. All rights reserved. Verses marked KJV are taken from the HOLY BIBLE: King James Version, © 1979, by Holman Bible Publishers. Verses marked LRB are taken from The Life Recovery BIBLE, © 1998, by Tyndale House Publishers, Inc.
Copyright © 2010 Arquila A. Todd
v3.0

Outskirts Press, Inc.
http://www.outskirtspress.com

ISBN: 978-1-4327-4141-9
ISBN: 978-1-4327-4142-6

Library of Congress Control Number: 2009930200

Outskirts Press and the "OP" logo are trademarks belonging to Outskirts Press, Inc.

PRINTED IN THE UNITED STATES OF AMERICA
Edited by Chandra Sparks Taylor www.chandrasparkstaylor.com and Alanna Boutin www.youreditress.com.
Cover designed by Kirk Simms kirk.simms@gmail.com

I would like to hear from you. Please send your thoughts and comments about this book to me at this address KinsmanRedeemer41@gmail.com. Thank you.

*This book is dedicated to my Heavenly Father,*
*Who has blessed me beyond measure.*

# Table of Contents

# Preface

My story parallels the story of the Prodigal Son in Luke 15. I left home, got my degree, and lived the life I wanted to live. Along the way, I made some really bad choices, which made my life a living hell. There was slop everywhere. My world was upside down, but then I came to my senses. I realized I had sinned against God. I went back to my Heavenly Father and asked for forgiveness. I knew He had something better for me than the way my life was going. My Father saw me coming and had compassion on me. He welcomed me home with outstretched arms. I wrapped my arms around His neck and held on for dear life. He celebrated my return home. I was once dead but am alive again. I was lost but now am found. I was blind, but now I see.

Maybe you can relate to going out from your Heavenly Father's house to make it on your own. You made some bad decisions along the way. You found slop all around you. Come to your senses. Your Father has the solutions to all your problems! Go home. Go back to your Father's house. He is waiting on you with outstretched arms, waiting to welcome you, His child, back home.

I want to share what I have learned. I love my sisters enough to want them to know the Biblical principals there are about dating. This book is meant to stop the pain and hurt that is associated with dating. This book is meant to clear up the disillusionments women experience.

One day I asked God, "Father, there must be something in Your Word that tells us how to date. Your Word is a lamp unto my feet and a light unto my path. I believe You will help me get the information out to Christian sisters in a way they can relate to. We can relate to Your Word. We can title the book in a way that will be receptive to women who love to read." So here we go.

I let God lead me. He wants to open our eyes and ears to His teachings. All we have to do is seek Him.

After my disastrous dating experience, I had a desire for Oprah Winfrey to do a series on dating. God said no. He said for me to stop looking for the answers in others. He said Oprah was doing what she was supposed to be doing. Now I was to be an answer. He told me to not fear the book writing process because He would be with me. He said He would see me through. His grace is sufficient. And I am a living testimony that it is.

So, if you see a problem and God gives you the solution, He is calling on you to be an answer to the problem for others as well as yourself. Do not fear. God will be with you.

After that, I walked out on faith. I would ask, "Lord, I don't understand why this happens in relationships. Lord, what does Your Word say about this?" In no time, God gave me the answers to my concerns. Every time, God proved Himself faithful. He is so amazing. I would sing and shout and dance. God gave me happy feet. There's nothing like it when God gives you happy feet. My cup runneth over. There's nothing like when God causes your cup to run over.

Try Him for yourself.

This book is what came out of the ashes of my relationships. My prayer is that God would use me, that He would use my experiences for His glory. My prayer is that you would get to know Him, that you would experience His love for you.

Please read this book and share what you learn with others. Reread it as often as necessary for your continued growth.

# 1

## Now That I've Got Your Attention!

I was in so much pain after my second failed relationship. *Enough was enough.* Something was wrong. I could feel it. There had to be a better way of falling in love and not being torn to pieces because a relationship did not work out. I fell on the floor in the fetal position and cried, "Lord, help me."

I had tried friends' advice. I had done what I thought would work. I had done what my ex had said to do. Nothing helped. Nothing worked. I went to the One who I knew had the solution to my situation. I knew He had the answers. I knew He had the key that would unlock the mystery to my misery.

And He answered my cry. God told me to be obedient. I was sinning by having sex outside of wedlock, and there was a price to pay—and boy, was it a big price. But I count that price joy because God didn't allow my pain to kill me. It drew me closer to Him. And that was my prayer: *Lord, don't let this kill me.*

The experience of lost love was unbearable. All I wanted was to have someone in my life who I could love, someone who would love me as much as I loved him. Isn't that what life is all about?

And the experience of another failed relationship was more than I could bear. I had loved my husband for eleven years, and my last two-and-a-half-year relationship had just ended. I couldn't and didn't understand what was wrong. I had loved them both. *Wasn't love enough?*

I knew I was a good person. I went to church, I gave, and I wasn't selfish. I had volunteered with Big Brothers Big Sisters for eleven years and with Meals-On-Wheels for three years. I paid my tithes, I read my Bible. What was missing? I prayed. I even fasted and prayed to ask God if the last guy I dated was the man for me. Before my mother had passed, she came to stay with me when I discovered she had Parkinson's and couldn't stay by herself. I took care of her when many kids would have put their parents in a nursing home. That was the least I could do for my mom.

Wasn't I entitled to a happy relationship? Why was this happening to me? Where was the love? Why wasn't it reciprocated? I cried over the lost love. I hated Charles, the guy I dated after my divorce, because our love had not materialized into a lifelong relationship. I felt confused, lost, and hurt all at the same time. I was depressed and just wanted life over. I wanted to go live with God, rather than remain in this horrible place. I prayed, *Lord, don't let this kill me. Lord, help me. I need You.* I cried and prayed, lying in the fetal position on my floor. God heard my cry. He told me my pain was because of my disobedience. I couldn't blame Charles for what I had done. I had put all of my love, hope, and trust in Charles. I had wanted him to be "the one." I had loved him and cared about him and shared myself with him. We were a couple, and a cute couple at that. What was wrong?

God said that I had put Charles first. I had loved him more than God. I had forsaken my first love. God wanted me to be happy and in love, but anything and anyone I put before Him would destroy me. And this relationship had taken its toll. He said I needed to love Him with all of my heart, soul, strength and mind. Instead, I had relied on Charles. I had put too much hope in him. *Lord, help me to never do that again.* I had to get my priorities straight. I was to love the Creator more than the creation. *Thank you, Lord, because nothing will separate me from Your love, not even my willful disobedience. You will allow the pain of my sin to hurt enough to drop me to my knees and have me come running to You.* This situation brought me to my knees, and there, I was able to listen to God's instructions for my life.

Next, He told me I needed to be obedient to Him in everything. I had been having premarital sex (fornication). God said my body was His and holy and I was to be a good steward over it. Well, I had not been obedient to His teachings about fornication, and I had to pay the price for that willful disobedience. Maybe Charles was the man for me, maybe not, but because I had chosen my way of doing things and not God's way, I was in the situation I found myself in. I had to take responsibility for my predicament. I couldn't blame anyone else. I knew better.

I had grown up in the church. But having sex with the guy I was dating is what I did. That willful disobedience had caught up with me, and I was sorry. I apologized to God for putting Charles first and for putting Antonio, my ex-husband, before Him. I also realized I had done that in my marriage. I had loved Antonio so much initially, and my misdirected love had caused me pain. My disobedience had caused me pain.

## CONFESS MY HURT

God showed me why my life was in such distress. He showed me how my self-esteem had been affected by my father's harsh words when I was growing up. My father had told me I would never be anything and I couldn't do anything right. I had told myself for years those words had made me the successful person I am. I had said to myself, *"I will show you."* I had a four-bedroom, three-bathroom home, a six-figure income, a car, and I vacationed and lived the life. One year, my husband and I vacationed in Hawaii and Jamaica and went snow skiing in Colorado. And we vacationed like this *every* year. But God showed me how my father's words were still affecting me. I was looking for the love from men that my father had never shown me. I was looking for a compliment my father rarely gave me. I was looking for approval my father rarely expressed. I was affected by my father's words more than I ever realized. I would do things just to prove I was good enough.

Once when I was in high school, I worked two summer jobs to prove I could make my own money. I joined the Army Reserves, applied for scholarships, and took out loans to show my father I could pay for college. I worked really hard in college and graduated with plans to become an air traffic controller. I desperately sought my father's approval, but never heard *"Good job, I'm proud of you."* I had to confess that my father's words had hurt and realize the extent of that injury.

God was getting to the root of my issues. God showed me that my motives for greeting most people were to feel a connection with them that I hadn't felt with my father. I was the one to make friends and be friendly. I was the lover of the bunch. I would give in hopes of people accepting me. I looked out for the underdog because I felt a need to protect. God showed me a myriad of motivations and the reasons why I did things the way I did. Self-examination and self-awareness are huge. They shed light on so many things.

## FORGIVE

God told me I needed to forgive my father because I had been forgiven. Forgiving my father would free me from being adversely affected and controlled even now by his harsh words. Matthew 18:18 tells us, "Whatever you bind on earth will be bound in heaven, and whatever you loose on earth will be loosed in heaven." To forgive my father would free me from the pain and misery of feeling like I didn't measure up. And forgiving my father would allow me to not imitate his same behavior.

So I asked, "How, Lord? How do I forgive the man who gave me life and was supposed to love me unconditionally?" God told me to pray for my father. Even though my father was deceased, I prayed for him. I prayed for God's love to touch my father. I prayed for his soul. I prayed for God's grace and mercy for my father. I prayed I could forgive him.

God showed me that my father had loved me. God brought to my remembrance all the wonderful fatherly things my father had done for me and my siblings. He had made us a playhouse in the backyard. He had built a tire swing in the front yard on which I have fond memories playing. He would make us homemade kites with newspaper, sticks, and string. He built us a swing on the front porch, and I still like to swing today.

My father taught me how to drive. He would check the oil and transmission fluid in my car when I had to travel. He did the best he could with what he had. Thinking about the good things allowed me to have a truer perspective of the way things were. I had concentrated so much on the negative that I had suppressed all of the positive things my father had done.

God told me I needed to consider my father's upbringing. Who knows what he went through growing up in Phenix City, Alabama, in the 1930s, '40s, and '50s? Who knows what harsh words were said to him? Who knows what someone said to make him feel bad about himself? People who have been hurt tend to hurt others. I prayed for his childhood and what he had been through, for God to have mercy.

Thank God that prayer changes things. I was able to forgive my father and love him. Mark 11:25–26 (KJV) says, "And when ye stand praying, forgive, if ye have ought against any: that your Father also which is in heaven may forgive you your trespasses. But if ye do not forgive, neither will your Father which is in heaven forgive your trespasses."

## GOD SHOWED ME, ME

God showed me where I had become like my father in my ways. Because I had not confessed the hurt that my father's words had caused, I had taken on those same characteristics myself. I had hurt others, especially my sister and my nieces and nephews. I could see my father's hurtful ways in my sister's behavior, but I had not seen them in my own. God showed me where often I had said very hurtful words to my sister and her kids. I was very critical and condescending. I was literally telling them what my father had told me: *"You will never measure up."* I had tried to control them by wanting them to do what I wanted them to do. I would criticize my sister for having kids out of wedlock and not having a job or any means to provide for them.

I have since learned criticizing does not help. I must edify, build up, and help her become the best person she can be. The best way to do that is to ask myself, "If she were me, what would I want someone to do for me?" The golden rule, according to Matthew 7:12 is, "So in everything, do to others what you would have them do unto you."

I would be really mean to my sister's children when they acted up. I was very harsh with my words and actions. I did do some things good for my sister but too often—much too often—I was my father's child. I would make condemning statements. I would be unloving and impatient. I also realize this was very much a part of a slave mentality—the practice of beating down someone who looks like me with words or actions. I had to be aware of the enemy and fight against his tricks with everything in me. He had caused enough havoc. Let the one who steals steal no more. Ephesians 6:4 teaches, "Fathers, do not exasperate your children; instead, bring them up in the training and instruction of the Lord." I was to teach them a better way instead of fussing at them.

These things stung me in my heart. I cried over the way I had treated my sister and her kids. It broke my heart to see the control I tried to will over her. I had feared becoming my father, and in a sense, I had done just what I feared. At one time, I had offered my sister money to have an abortion—to abort my beautiful nephew. Lord, how sorry I am for that. I was heartily sorrowful for my actions because I love my sister and her kids, but at the time, I hadn't been very loving. I called her and with tears running down my face asked her to forgive me for my harsh words and treatment. I told her God was working on me and showing me my shortcomings and to be patient with me because He was not through with me yet. I would be a better auntie. I had seen the error of my ways and wanted to do better. God told me to be more encouraging. I was to tell the kids I loved them and was proud of them and that they were beautiful and to pray with them and read Bible stories with them and to ask them to forgive me.

And I did ask them for forgiveness. Once I did, it felt like a weight lifted off my chest. I felt relieved and less burdened. I felt instantly better.

## GOD SHOWED ME MY SINS OF THE PAST

I had to deal with each of my sins and shortcomings on a heartfelt level. It is true that the truth shall set you free. I admitted to myself and the Father that I had done some pretty sinful things, for which I was now heartily sorrowful. I had never dealt with my sin, and saw it for the terrible thing it was. The awareness went something like this:

I had had two abortions that I felt at the time were justified because 1) I was in college, 2) the father of my kids was married, 3) the world was becoming wiser and weaker and I didn't want my children part of an increasingly sinful world, 4) I didn't want to lose my cute shape and be fat like so many women I saw every day, 5) I didn't want my lifestyle to change, 6) I saw people who had children and were so frustrated with them that I didn't want the headache of dealing with those frustrations. I thought I was making a good decision for me and for them.

After I recognized my sins in light of a Holy God who requires me to be holy, I repented and asked God to forgive me for killing His children, my blessings. I prayed He would forgive me for my lack of faith in Him, now knowing that He would have used them for His glory and made them wise in spite of the world. I prayed they would forgive me. With tears flowing from my eyes, I asked my children to forgive me for killing them and not letting them live and having a chance.

I had been mean to my stepdaughter. She was beautiful, and I was threatened by her presence. I didn't want her receiving the love from her father that belonged to me. Thank God for maturity. I now know that there is enough love for all of us. I am not in competition. But I was mean to her. Her hair was long and wavy. When it was time to comb it, I was much too rough. I would not have combed my hair like that. Now *that* is the test to see if you are out of order with your behavior: Ask yourself if you would want someone to do to you what you have done to them? I had combed her hair hard until she was in tears. I was not patient. I did not put myself in her shoes and treat her the way I would have wanted to be treated if someone were combing my hair.

In my heart I asked her to forgive me. One day when I get the chance, I will ask her in person to forgive me. I spanked her too hard. I should have been kinder and more patient. I wasn't all bad, but I had committed sins against others that I had not dealt with. I had committed them and just went on with my life. This was a time of reflection and confession and asking for forgiveness and forgiving myself. God had shown me where I had done much for her and her brother throughout their lives. I was not always mean. I did wise up and do much better, and I was thankful for that.

We all have a past. I thank God for growth, maturity, and wisdom. I thank Him that my past does not dictate my future. I thank my Father that I am not shackled to what I have done, but God has given me freedom through confession and repentance.

I slept with my ex-husband's best friend—and his wife and I were friends. God showed me how my selfishness could have been disastrous for them. I was so concerned about me and what I was going through at the time that I hadn't considered what I was doing to a family. God had me look at the situation from her viewpoint, and it dropped me to my knees to think that my friend could have slept with my husband. I had never looked at my infidelity that way. My God, what a revelation! It hurt me deeply when I thought of my deception and selfishness. I was heartily sorrowful. Before, I had justified what I had done. I said he was what I needed at the time and she didn't deserve him, but God held me accountable, and I knew better and was sorry for my willful disobedience. I had sinned against God. I saw myself for the wretched person I am. I need grace and mercy.

God did not tell me to go to them and apologize, so I did it in my heart, but I know when the time comes, I will have to ask for forgiveness. Second Corinthians 13:5 (KJV) tells us, "Examine yourselves, whether ye be in the faith; prove your own selves. Know ye not your own selves, how that Jesus Christ is in you, except ye be reprobates?"

At that time in my life, my mother was ill and she would stay with my brother for six months, and the plan was for her to stay with me and my husband for six months. We would share in taking care of her. Well, when I had the conversation with my husband, he said she could only stay for three months. And there was no discussing it. As far as he was concerned, the matter was settled. I couldn't understand; I didn't understand. My mother had been nice and kind to him, his children, and his family. She needed us now more than ever, and he was saying no to six months of care.

You can hurt me, but not my momma. I had never felt so low. All of the intimacy had left my marriage. I felt no connection to him. I was in so much pain. My feelings of love for him had been destroyed over the years by his constant criticism and condemnation, so I found refuge in another man's arms. God said I should have found refuge in His arms. There were no excuses.

## WHAT I LEARNED ABOUT CONFESSING AND TAKING A LOOK AT MYSELF

God loves me unconditionally. Even with all the bad things I have done, God still loves me and can use me to help others. He does not condemn me, He makes me over. Hallelujah! Moses killed an Egyptian, and God used him to deliver the Israelites out of Egypt, so no matter what you have done, come as you are. He is an accepting God. He is a forgiving God. He is a loving God. God loves the person but hates the sin. I also learned that when I took a real look at myself and saw the wretch that I am, I have no right to be judgmental with anyone else. It was only God's grace and mercy that has seen me through. Now I must show that same grace and mercy to others through understanding that He so graciously has shown to me. According to First John 1:9, "If we confess our sins, he is faithful and just and will forgive us our sins and purify us from all unrighteousness." God cleaned me. He washed me and took out the impurities.

Are there some unconfessed sins from *your* past for which you need to ask forgiveness? Are there hurts from your past that are still affecting you today? Ask God to show you. Ask God to help you. He wants to. Your failures will never diminish God's love for you.

## SELF-EVALUATION

"A man ought to examine himself" (First Corinthians 11:28a). The act of self-evaluation, confessing my sins, asking for forgiveness, and sinning no more freed me. It was like all of the sin was dirt piled on top of me, separating me from God and life. The dirt—sin— had blanketed me, and I was in a grave—darkness and despair. But as I confessed and asked for forgiveness and walked in obedience, layers of dirt were removed until I could see and feel the light and experience God's love and forgiveness. We were closer, we were so much closer.

I thanked Him that the experience had not killed me. I thanked Him that nothing will separate me from Him, not even me. I thanked Him that everything works for the good of those who love the Lord and are called according to His purpose (Romans 8:28). All of this worked out for my good and God's glory. Before, I was so twisted that I couldn't see straight. My sin had me twisted and just existing. Now I had a new walk and a new talk. Galatians 6:15 says, "Neither circumcision nor uncircumcision means anything; what counts is a new creation." To God be the glory.

Is your life all it could be? Have you been hurt, or are you frustrated with how your relationships are going? All you have to do is ask God to help you. Jesus came to save us from eternal separation from the Father because of our sins. He stands at the door of your heart and knocks, just waiting for an opportunity to come in and sit with you. Will you invite Him in?

I had a girlfriend say to me, "I thought I was farther along than that." In essence, what she was saying is she had been in church all of her life. Why was she still making such baby Christian mistakes? First, she needed to understand that all have sinned and fallen short of His glory (Romans 3:23). Second, she needed to stop fooling herself about the mistakes she was making and sins she was committing—because she wasn't fooling God. She was living in denial of her wretchedness. He sees her shortcomings and loves her anyway. Our rightness will never get us into heaven. That's why we need the blood of the Lamb.

If you are like my friend, thinking you are farther along in your Christian walk than you are but still making mistakes, admit you are in need of a savior. Admit you can't do it by yourself. John 15:5 says, "I am the vine; you are the branches. If a man remains in me and I in him, he will bear much fruit; apart from me you can do nothing." Admit that you sin against God and need His Spirit to work in you to get things right. Christian maturity is a *process*. Don't get down on yourself. It's a process. Be patient with yourself. God can work it out.

Mark 2:16–17 (KJV) says, "And when the scribes and Pharisees saw him eat with publicans and sinners, they said unto his disciples, How is it that he eateth and drinketh with publicans and sinners? When Jesus heard it, he saith unto them, They that are whole have no need of the physician, but they that are sick: I came not to call the righteous, but sinners to repentance." Jesus came to heal us and make us whole.

# 2

# My Testimony

I was reading *Purpose Driven Life* by Rick Warren. All of the chapters had in one way or another inspired me, but Chapter 31 spoke to my spirit in such a way that I felt compelled to tell my story.

The author wrote:

> You have been shaped by your experiences in life, most of which were beyond your control. God allowed them for His purpose of molding you. In determining your shape for serving God, you should examine at least six kinds of experiences from your past: family experiences, educational experiences, vocational experiences, spiritual experiences, ministry experiences, and painful experiences. It is the last category, painful experiences, that God uses the most to prepare you for ministry. God never wastes a hurt! In fact, your greatest ministry will most likely come out of your greatest hurt. Who could better help an alcoholic recover than someone who fought that demon and found freedom? Only shared experiences can help others.

Why, you ask, do I share my testimony? Because I don't want

another sister, mother, daughter, or friend to have to learn this lesson the way I did. Plus, my Father God tells me to share.

So here is my experience:

I would be on my knees praying when the phone would ring. I would cut that prayer off to answer the phone, hoping it was Charles. That is how far I had fallen in love with this man. I would have plans with my girlfriends for Friday night, and he would call. There went my plans with my friends. I put him first. Then one day, things changed. He would make plans for us to go somewhere or do something, and the plans never came to fruition. He came over the morning of Valentine's Day, just to go missing that evening. And at the end of the relationship, he would claim his cell phone didn't work and he didn't get my calls. Now mind you, it wasn't always this crazy. The relationship started off beautifully. We would be walking down the steps of my three-floor apartment, and he would turn around on each step to give me a passionate kiss. If it was raining, he would get my car from under the shed and pull it next to the walkway for me before I went to work. He cut my catheter when it needed to be cut after my hysterectomy. He bought me sherbet and ginger ale when I was sick. I met his family—his mother, sisters, daughter, and grandson. The man was caring, thoughtful, and smart. He made sure I had a cell phone charger in my car so I wouldn't be without phone service.

When I finally allowed myself to fall in love with this man, I fell hard and without conditions, without limits. I aimed to please. We were a couple, and I wanted to do couple things. I wanted to spend more time with him and one day get married. As I look back, there came a time when I made him my god. This was the biggest mistake of my life. We all know God is a jealous God and will let us see we can't depend on anything we put before Him.

# MY TESTIMONY

## MY LIFE LESSON

At the time, I couldn't understand what happened to us and why, because we were the perfect couple, both beautiful with good-paying jobs and at one time had loved each other very much. Now he was missing in action. My heart was broken, and I fell to my knees and asked God to help me. There was no interrupting these prayers for help. I lay there on the floor, in my tears, hurting so bad, asking my Father God to help me. He knew I depended on Him, and He had mercy. God heard my cries and blessed me with some life lessons.

My biggest mistake was to put my hope for love, security, joy, and trust in a man. Now don't get me wrong, God wants us to be in happy relationships, but we must seek Him first. No other relationship can do for us what God can do. Only God can fulfill us and heal us and make us whole. Charles was six-four, handsome, and smart. He was a supervisor at the center where I worked. If I had a problem with someone there, I would tell him about it. I knew the guys there respected him and wouldn't mess with me for fear of him.

With more and more things, I gradually put my dependence in him instead of taking my concerns to the Father. Too often, I relied on Charles instead of God. Too often, I made time for him instead of God. Charles came first. I remember having plans to go with my girlfriend to a singles conference at Oak Cliff Bible Fellowship Church one weekend. We had made plans, the money was paid, and then Charles called and wanted to spend the weekend at my timeshare. There went my plans to go to the singles conference. I put him first. It all happened so gradually. Initially, I was busy and happy doing my thing with my friends. The more time I spent with him, the more I enjoyed his company—until one day I looked up and I had changed.

My behavior said he was the center of my world. I waited to see what we were going to do for the weekend. I waited until he called to make sure he wouldn't have plans for us before I decided to do something else. I wasn't like this initially. And looking back on it, I see now where he liked me and was attracted to me because I had a life that didn't center around him. As soon as he became the center of my life, he began to take me for granted. I was too available! I was there no matter what. Believe it or not, we can be *too* available for our male companions. He felt he had me, so it was not necessary to work so hard to see me because I was always available. Why work hard when I was making it easy for him?

I had to make a choice to put God first, as it tells us in Luke 12:30–31 (KJV), "For all these things do the nations of the world seek after: and your Father knoweth that ye have need of these things. But rather seek ye the kingdom of God; and all these things shall be added unto you." I had to seek God through daily reading of His Word and praying about every situation. If you don't believe the Word of God, ask Him to increase your faith and He will.

Love, fear, trust—these are words of worship. Jesus commands us to love God, fear God, and trust God only. Matthew 22:37 (KJV) says, "Jesus said unto him, Thou shalt love the Lord thy God with all thy heart, and with all thy soul, and with all thy mind."

Anytime we long for something apart from God, fear something more than God, or trust in something other than God to make us happy, fulfilled, or secure, we worship a false god. As a result, we deserve the judgment and wrath of the true God.

Exodus 20:1–6 (KJV) tells us what God wants us to know about putting Him first versus having idols.

> And God spake all these words, saying, I am the Lord thy God, which have brought thee out of the land of Egypt, out of the house of bondage. Thou shalt have no other

gods before me. Thou shalt not make unto thee any graven image, or any likeness of any thing that is in heaven above, or that is in the earth beneath, or that is in the water under earth. Thou shalt not bow down thyself to them, nor serve them: for I the Lord thy God am a jealous God, visiting the iniquity of the fathers upon the children unto the third and fourth generation of them that hate me; And showing mercy unto thousands of them that love me, and keep my commandments.

It was God, and He alone, who has brought us out of whatever bondage we have experienced in the past. And if you are still in bondage, only God can bring you out. He may use others to assist in the process, but all blessings come from Him. Praise God from whom all blessings flow. Praise Him above ye heavenly host. Praise Him Father, Son, and Holy Ghost.

Idolatry occurs when a person removes God from His rightful place of supremacy and puts something or someone else in that place. God loves us and desires our highest good. He made us for Himself. Nothing—no person, no object—is to take His rightful place in our affections or our attention. Think about it. Does He have dominance in your affections? Do you desire Him above all else and everyone else? Could you live without anyone *but* Him? Or have others—idols—crowded Him out so that you live for others above Him, seeking to please them above your God? And what priority do you give God? How much of your attention does He receive?

I can tell you for sure I had put this man before God. Whom do you seek to spend most of your time with—your Heavenly Father or the guy you are dating? Are you desperate for a man or for God? What is God trying to tell you about what you are doing? He is trying to get your attention. God wants us to return to Him. Job

22:23 says, "If you return to the Almighty, you will be restored: If you remove wickedness far from your tent."

I was so twisted. But God!

God called me to be obedient to His will and purpose for my life. Instead, I was obeying God when it was convenient for me (i.e., not stealing, but I was fornicating—having sex out of wedlock). I went to church, but I left church and went and got in bed with Charles. I knew better. God's Holy Spirit was convicting me. I felt bad about what I was doing, but I dismissed that feeling. There were times when we would be making love and I would thank God for how good it felt. I had not thought of how bad the consequences would feel. I was living in the moment for that instant gratification, never thinking of the pain my choices would cause me.

But there was pain for my disobedience. Charles would disrespect me. He would take me for granted. He would go missing, and I would wonder where he was and who he was with. I remember breaking up with him on several occasions, just to find myself back with him. He would flirt with women right in front of me. I would wonder, is this normal? See, I had been married for ten years and wasn't sure what dating looked like since I hadn't done it in so long. God told me I had brought this disrespect on myself but to rest assured, all of this had happened to draw me closer to the Father who could love me like I needed to be loved. No other person could do that for me. And now I am a living testimony to God's goodness and grace. He is all we need. Because when we have Him, we have everything else.

Romans 8:28 tells us, "... all things God works for the good of those who love him, who have been called according to his purpose." This worked for my good. I grew.

I decided to dedicate my body to God, to be obedient, to live according to His will and way for my life. I said "yes" to His will, "yes" to His way, and I haven't been happier or more full of joy and living in peace than I can ever remember. My body belongs to the Lord, and I need to be a good steward of it. God was trying to tell me something. He was trying to get my attention.

I had only known one friend who was practicing abstinence. The concept seemed foreign. Everybody was having sex while dating. I had grown up in the church and rarely did someone not have sex. It was almost unheard of. I wasn't taught as a child to value my body and that my body belongs to God and men would respect me more if I said no to their sexual advances. Well, I thank God for showing me the more excellent way. His way is medicine to a sick soul. His way is resurrection to a dead person walking. We see dead people walking every day. Sometimes *we* are the dead walking. I was.

I thank God for showing me a better way. He showed me the importance of saying no to sex before marriage. I do not want to share myself with numerous men and have nothing special for my husband because I had done it all with other men I had dated. I didn't want to have sex with a guy I was dating and then wonder who else he was having sex with or if we were going to get married. I wasn't going to have sex with another man who wasn't my husband so we could break up and I would regret ever having slept with him because he didn't deserve me and my precious body. I was not going to risk catching a sexually transmitted disease. God told me to be abstinent because He loves me, not because He wanted to deprive me of something special. Sharing my body is meant for one someone special. And I thank Him for showing me the importance of that.

And men will try me. I will be tempted, but I ask God for help. I asked Him to increase my faith in Him so I would believe Him when He told me to be obedient so that I would enjoy long life and things would go well for me. Deuteronomy 6:3a says, "Hear,

O Israel, and be careful to obey so that it may go well with you and that you may increase greatly."

It is time for a change. Change needs to happen if you desire a different outcome. I was ready for a change. I didn't want the same mistakes from my last marriage to plague my new relationships. I wanted to learn the lesson and grow.

When I was growing up, no one told me I was fearfully and wonderfully made. No one told me not to seek affirmation from other people but to seek God's Word, which tells me who I am and whose I am. I had to renew my mind by meditating on His words.

Psalm 139:14 says, "I praise you because I am fearfully and wonderfully made; your works are wonderful, I know that full well."

First Peter 2:9 says, "But you are a chosen people, a royal priesthood, a holy nation, a people belonging to God."

God made me unique. According to Psalm 139:15, "My frame was not hidden from you when I was made in the secret place."

God made me one of a kind. Revelation 4:11 says, "You are worthy, our Lord and God, to receive glory and honor and power, for you created all things, and by your will they were created and have their being."

God made me special. Ephesians 1:11 reads, "In him we were also chosen, having been predestined according to the plan of him who works out everything in conformity with the purpose of his will."

God made me in His image. Genesis 1:26–27 says, "Then God said, 'Let us make man in our image, in our likeness, and let them rule over the fish of the sea and the birds of the air, over the livestock, over all the earth, and over all the creatures that move along the ground.' So God created man in his own image, in the image of God he created him; male and female he created them."

# MY TESTIMONY

God doesn't make mistakes. Deuteronomy 32:4 reveals, "He is the Rock, his works are perfect, and all his ways are just. A faithful God who does no wrong, upright and just is he."

If you don't like the creation, talk to the Creator! Isaiah 44:2 says, "This is what the Lord says—he who made you, who formed you in the womb, and who will help you: do not be afraid."

I love me and accept me because of who God made me! Ephesians 1:3–5 reads, "Praise be to the God and Father of our Lord Jesus Christ, who has blessed us in the heavenly realms with every spiritual blessing in Christ. For he chose us in him before the creation of the world to be holy and blameless in his sight. In love he predestined us to be adopted as his sons [and daughters] through Jesus Christ, in accordance with his pleasure and will" (brackets added).

It does not matter what you say about me, only what God says. Acts 10:34–35 tells us, "Then Peter began to speak: 'I now realize how true it is that God does not show favoritism but accepts men from every nation who fear him and do what is right.'"

I am not above you, and I am not below you. Romans 10:12 says, "For there is no difference between Jew and Gentile [Black or White]—the same Lord is Lord of all and richly blesses all who call on him" (brackets added).

I am worth more than rubies. Proverbs 31:10 says, "She is worth far more than rubies."

I cried for that little girl who did not know her worth. I cried because no one had told me that I was precious and a princess. At times, I had had sexual experiences just because the guy I was dating wanted to. I didn't think of how valuable I was at the time because no one had ever told me I was special or valuable or that God's Spirit lives in me! I was told I would never be anything and I couldn't do anything right. My father would only tell me how pretty

# MY TESTIMONY

I was after I put on my Sunday best and twirled in front of him, asking if I was pretty, and he would say, "Yes, baby."

I look back on those days of having sex with guys I barely cared about, and I see how truly mistaken I was not to value myself. I hadn't valued my body. I had no reason to. I wasn't told I was supposed to. But I thank God I know better now. It was not my fault I didn't know any better. I would not let my past confine me nor define me. I would not live being ruled by my past mistakes. I became celibate. I dedicated my body to God. It was not too late. I vowed from this day I would value myself and not sleep around. I choose to do what's right. I am too valuable to pass myself around from man to man. It's not too late to change. It's never too late as long as you have breath to start doing things God's way! Start today, dedicate today! Say "yes" to God's will and "yes" to God's way.

I didn't understand I was giving men something very special. I cried because that little girl was special, and she didn't know it. And when my tears were finished, I thanked God He had shared His truth with me, and He told me to share the truth with you so you can share it with your daughters, sisters, friends, and nieces.

We often put one another down, like when we are "only kidding." But there is power in words, and we have to be careful about what we say. We are to tell the females in our lives how unique they are. We are to tell them God made them in His image. We are to tell them He designed them before the earth was formed. He made them perfect, because God doesn't make mistakes. It doesn't matter what other races say or even your own race, it only matters what God says. If that little girl in each of us respects herself, then others will respect her. But she *has* to first respect herself and love herself.

I had to replace the thoughts I had about myself.

Romans 12:1–2 (KJV) says, "I beseech you therefore, brethren, by the mercies of God, that ye present your bodies a living sacrifice, holy, acceptable unto God, which is your reasonable service. And be not conformed to this world: but be ye transformed by the renewing of your mind, that ye may prove what is that good, and acceptable, and perfect, will of God."

I had to renew my mind.

God showed me where I was addicted to the approval of others. God wants us to know when we value what others think above what He thinks. How can you tell if you are an approval addict?

The definition of an approval addict is someone who is motivated by what others think to the point where what others think controls his or her behavior. Are you disappointed when you're not included in an activity others are participating in to the point you change your behavior just to fit in? Do you smile when you have nothing to smile about? Do you laugh at jokes that aren't funny? Do you speak to people who are rude, mean, and treat you badly in hopes that one day they will not behave this way toward you? Does it hurt your feelings when someone does not speak or acknowledge you? Or do you think, *Oh well. No problem, that's their choice.*

If you wear your favorite clothes, drive a nice car, live in a fine house, but someone does not acknowledge your accomplishments, does it upset you? Can you do a good deed, not get the recognition for it, and be fine about that, or does it ruin your day? Do you have to be in the spotlight or you won't have anything to do with the project? Are you able to tell someone God's truth about a matter, even though they may become frustrated at you and bring some distance in the relationship, or do you go along to get along with no dissension with what they are saying?

Do you look around to see what others are thinking about what you are doing? Do you base your actions on what they think? If someone ignores you, does it bother you?

# MY TESTIMONY

If you answered "yes" to any of these questions, ask God if you seek the approval of others instead of His approval, and to help you deal with your approval addiction so He can heal you. God is trying to show us what is in our hearts that is not of Him. You can then be free from the bondage of what other people think, and you will be able to believe what God has said about you. That is: *HE LOVES YOU UNCONDITIONALLY.* God frees us so we can worship Him. What is hindering *your* worship? Exodus 8:20 says, "Then the Lord said to Moses, 'Get up early in the morning and confront Pharaoh as he goes to the water and say to him, "This is what the Lord says: Let my people go, so that they may worship me.""

God showed me that even when I was a teenager I wanted the approval of my peers. I remember my first sexual experience. I was dating a really nice guy. He had had sex. It seemed all of my friends had had sex. It was the popular thing to do. I remember feeling embarrassed because I had yet to experience what everyone was talking about. I lied to my boyfriend, telling him I was experienced. To be considered a virgin, I thought, would put me in the outcast department, so I took matters into my own hands. I asked a friend's older brother to have sex with me. He had no qualms about it. We had sex. It hurt and was awful. My first experience was with someone I didn't care about, who didn't care about me.

I tell you this so you can talk to your daughters, sisters, and nieces about what they may possibly be going through. They may be thinking, to fit in, they need to give up "the precious." Tell them, *NO WAY!*

# 3

# **Healing**

I became obedient to the Bible's teaching of abstinence so I could live under God's blessings instead of the curses that were plaguing my life because of my choice to be disobedient. I was sick and tired of the distress in my life. I needed a change, so I surrendered—I yielded ownership and relinquished control over what I considered mine—my body. I had to surrender my life, marital status, relationships, past and purity.

I MUST SURRENDER MY LIFE. Matthew 16:24 says, "Then Jesus said unto his disciples, 'If anyone would come after me, he must deny himself and take up his cross and follow me.'"

I must accept God's driving habits and directions. Where I am right now, being single, is God's place for me for this season. I am to live and obey and love and believe right here. God, not your marital status, defines your life. I was so concerned with dating and getting married that I wasn't giving myself a chance to enjoy being single.

I MUST SURRENDER MY MARITAL STATUS. Whatever God says for me about me being married or single is what is for me. This doesn't mean I do not desire to be married, because I do, but I accept where He has me. God wants to guide us in our relationships like He guided the Israelites. We often pray for His guidance in career matters or health issues. Well, God wants us to seek His guidance in our relationships as well.

I MUST SURRENDER MY RELATIONSHIPS. I will only date believers. We are to be *equally* yoked. The illustration of being yoked is that of cattle having harnesses around their necks that lead them in the same direction. I want to be harnessed with a man going in the same direction God is leading me. I am to watch his actions to make sure he isn't just talking a good game. I will not shack up. Hebrews 13:4 says, "Marriage should be honored by all, and the marriage bed kept pure, for God will judge the adulterer and all the sexually immoral."

Keep yourself pure. Develop your prayer life. Pray prayers of direction and detection. I pray, "Lord, your will be done," and, "Lord, guide my feet."

I had to understand that whoever God has for me is the one for me. It might not be Charles. It's not for me to choose. I want God's choice for my life. Nehemiah 9:12 states, "By day you led them with a pillar of cloud, and by night with a pillar of fire to give them light on the way they were to take." Our Heavenly Father wants to guide us in the way we should take regarding our relationships. When we don't follow His lead, we find ourselves in stressful places.

I HAD TO SURRENDER MY PAST. Let it go. Philippians 3:13–14 says, "Brothers, I do not consider myself yet to have taken hold of it. But one thing I do: Forgetting what is behind and straining toward what is ahead, I press on toward the goal to win the prize for which God has called me heavenward in Christ Jesus."

I vowed not to stay stuck and to forgive myself, learn the lesson, and grow. I would not beat myself up over my mistakes in the past.

God said no condemnation, so I decided I would not condemn myself, nor would I let others condemn me. Romans 8:1–4 says,

> Therefore, there is now no condemnation for those who are in Christ Jesus, because through Christ Jesus the law of the Spirit of life set me free from the law of sin and death. For what the law was powerless to do in that it was weakened by the sinful nature, God did by sending his own Son in the likeness of sinful man to be a sin offering. And so he condemned sin in sinful man, in order that the righteous requirements of the law might be fully met in us, who do not live according to the sinful nature but according to the Spirit.

I faced the hurt and pain and unfair treatment I had experienced in each relationship. I remembered Jesus had suffered on the cross, and He was innocent. I remembered He said to God, the Father, in Luke 23:34 (KJV), "Father, forgive them; for they know not what they do." It was important for me to forgive those who had hurt me and had been unfair toward me. Jesus had done nothing wrong, and He chose to forgive. It would behoove us to follow after our big brother and forgive those who have hurt us.

I MUST SURRENDER MY PURITY. First Thessalonians 4:3–8 says,

> It is God's will that you should be sanctified [set apart]: that you should avoid sexual immorality; that each of you should learn to control his own body in a way that is holy and honorable, not in passionate lust like the heathen, who do not know God; and that in this matter no one should wrong his brother or take advantage of him. The Lord will punish men for all such sins, as we have already told you and warned you. For God did not call us to be impure, but

to live a holy life. Therefore, he who rejects this instruction does not reject man but God, who gives you his Holy Spirit (brackets added).

When we have sex outside of marriage, we sin against ourselves, our brother, and God our Father. And God punishes us for our sinful choices.

The pain of the relationship with Charles had left me depressed and out of sorts. I had to do something to get out of my depression. I remember praising God through songs. I would put my gospel CDs in my car CD player and that would be all I would listen to. Then at home, I would also listen to my gospel music. I would cry, sing, and praise God for His goodness. Then I would read books that blessed me.

I was thirsty for a better way. I was desperate for knowledge and understanding. God blessed me with one book after another written by authors who had been blessed, and they shared with me what they knew, what they had learned, and I am thankful.

I meditated. I opened myself up to hear from God. I positioned myself to hear from God. If He spoke, fine; if not, it would not be because I was too busy to listen. I just wanted to practice being still and quiet so I could hear His voice and know His will for my life.

I became quiet in my everyday dealings. I assumed a posture of listening, not only to Him but to others as well. Everyone can teach me something, if I only listen.

I realized the importance of allowing God to pour His blessing into me. I needed Him to fill me up with His words. I needed to study the Bible, listen to His Spirit, meditate, and walk and talk with Him and increase my prayer time. "The Lord is in his holy temple; let all the earth be silent before him" (Habakkuk 2:20). I was glad when they said unto me, let us go into the house of the Lord.

I realized I needed me and God-time. There had to be a balance.

There is a time for everything under the sun. There is a time to be Mary, sitting at the feet of Jesus, listening to what He has to say, and Martha, busy doing the work that needs to get done. But balance is so important. If you haven't spent the necessary time at the feet of Jesus listening to Him to know your purpose and His will for your life, how can you know what to do? What's important? What matters? What are your kingdom-building responsibilities? Only what we do for the kingdom will last.

Mary was at the feet of Jesus, listening to what He had to say. That is vital for our lives as well. Do you listen to God? In our quiet time is where we get the answers to life's problems, we get the jobs to perform, we get our assignments. And if God has given you an assignment, He will give you the provisions whereby to carry them out, so your life's work won't be in vain. You won't be anxious and worried. Are you doing what you should? God will tell you what you should do. He will be your guide and your provider. What a wonderful Father we have. He will show you which job is yours and which spouse is yours. He will make a way and provide for you. Your strength will lie in Him and what He can do with and through you, which is *everything*. Luke 1:37 (KJV) tells us, "For with God nothing shall be impossible."

Then after God has poured into you, you can pour into others. You will know who to give your pearls to. You will know which land to occupy and thereby receive your inheritance because He has instructed you. You will know which words to say to help a friend in his time of conflict or difficulty, and your words will be profound because they will be God's words. You will have an understanding of why people are the way they are and why situations happen the way they do because you have asked the Father and He has revealed it to you. Or you will say, "Lord, You know," and as long as He knows, that is good enough.

# MY TESTIMONY

God wanted me to depend on Him and not anyone else. You see, I would walk around, speaking to people whom I came into contact with. Not that this is a bad thing, but I did it out of fear—fear of not being accepted. I needed connections and felt slighted if someone did not return my hello or kind words. I was looking for affirmation. I wanted to feel worthy. God told me to keep my head up because I often walked with my head down, looking at the ground. He said to keep my eyes on Him and look to the hills from which cometh my help, my help cometh from the Lord (Psalm 121:1–2). There were times when I didn't get it right, but I practiced. I tried hard not to look into the faces of others and see their disapproving looks and their accusatory glances. They could see the longing on my face, the longing of wanting to be included and loved and connected. They would sometimes exclude me because of my obvious desire to be included or prejudice. God showed me where I had Him and didn't need anybody else. He showed me that if someone didn't want to include me—fine, that was their choice. I would be okay with not being included because I didn't want to be where I was not welcomed. I have all I need in Him.

As a matter of fact, for a season, I stopped speaking altogether. He was showing me how people had once spoken to me and now if I didn't speak to them first, they would not speak. It was as if they included me by speaking, and now it was up to me to maintain the relationship. It was up to me to make every connection after their initial one. Their appearance of being friendly and inviting was just an illusion. It was fake inclusion. When I didn't speak, their attitudes were like, *"What? She didn't speak to me? How dare she not give me the courtesy and proper addressing that I am due? Doesn't she know who I am?"*

God showed me where I had an inferiority complex that was fueled by people who wanted me to elevate them and make them feel important. They wanted me to feel what they said was the way things were and not think for myself. They wanted me to affirm them. Well, God told me to have no other god before Him, so me worshipping others had to stop. Me seeking others' approval had to stop. Me feeling inferior had to stop. Me being affected by what other people did or did not do had to stop! I am referring to what they thought that didn't match up to what God thought.

After becoming aware of this issue, I took this stance: No more defining myself by what other people think about me. God would define me. What He thought mattered. I had to get my thinking straight. People—White, Mexican, Black, Chinese—only feel superior when we make them feel that way. We take our power back by not affirming others. I was to stop elevating them to a status of more than they were. No one is above me. A person can feel special or superior, but I don't have to feel that they are, and I choose to feel that they aren't. I choose not to elevate anyone above the status of everyday human. No one is better than anyone else. I as a Black female denounce all labels of my race because of someone's fear of us, to keep us below them. Their opinion of me is not my reality. Their opinion isn't worth a hill of beans. Only God's opinion matters, and if someone of my own race had a derogatory opinion that does not line up with the word of God, they are dismissed as well.

You know, I have my lips puckered and my hands on my hips and my neck rotating ever so slightly. (Don't miss your opportunity to shout.)

Now I have God. I don't fear losing any false, fake relationships because they weren't valued relationships in the first place. They were conditional relationships. They were based on the condition that I make the other person feel superior. No more of that. God told me to live in peace, not to kiss anyone's butt. The more I depended on God, the less I depended on others. And God will always be with me because in Hebrews 13:5, He has promised to never leave me nor forsake me.

Some of the people left the relationship, or whatever you call it, because I didn't need their approval. I didn't fear them not speaking to me, and I stopped trying to be included in their circle. I was no longer elevating them. Exclusion no longer bothered me. I walked with my head up with the confidence of having God in me and He being my Father and I His child, and He gave me His words to help me along the way. God is no respecter of persons (Acts 10:34, KJV). I am fearfully and wonderfully made (Psalms 139:14), and to fear no man, but God who can send me to hell (Luke 12:5).

God took away everything I had depended on and thought I needed so I could depend on Him alone. He wanted me to see I could only depend on Him. He, alone, is from everlasting to everlasting.

I was taking medicine that jeopardized my job. I had defined myself by my job. I was proud to be an air traffic controller. God showed me what it would feel like to lose my job when I thought I would lose it because of my illness and the medications I had to take. He showed me how my job could be taken away, and then where would I be? How would I feel about myself? I would be the same person. I felt I couldn't live without my cell phone. On several occasions, I would accidently leave my phone at home. I had no time to go back and get it. After going all day without my phone, I could see that having it wasn't necessary. Who knew?

I would forget my watch, and I felt I needed to have my watch. God had me turn off the TV. Before, I had turned the TV on as soon as my feet hit the floor in the morning and I watched it all day. I had never thought of going without watching TV for an entire day. Now God showed me where depending on these aforementioned things were misplaced dependencies.

My family didn't call as much. My friends didn't call as much. It was like God was putting me on an island to show me He was all I needed—everything and everyone else was extra. I didn't even feel I needed to watch the weather. God would take care of me.

I let my hair go gray, its natural color. I let my perm grow out to allow my hair to be natural. I didn't care what others thought. God made it nappy, and I was okay with it being nappy. I let the hair on my legs grow. I had shaved the hair on my legs because of fear of what others would say if the hair grew. I was changing from living by the world's standards.

There were even people who I called friends who saw my growth and didn't want to have anything to do with me. As long as I was complaining and gossiping about my relationships, they were there. But as soon as my metamorphosis was taking place, they wouldn't have anything to do with my maturity. It was as if they were codependent on my misery. God removed those toxic relationships, and I was thankful.

When I stopped being the one who was always seeking approval, the one engaging and speaking because I was no longer desperate to be included, people's real colors came out. They wanted to know, "What's going on with her?"

Well, I was growing in strength in God, and the growth felt good. There came balance in my relationships, even with my girlfriends. I started to notice the dynamics of those relationships. I paid attention to who was doing all of the legwork and who was not. I paid attention to how much I called them and how often they called me. I noticed that sometimes I would call and it would be months later before I would get a call from some of them.

I started to make the relationships more balanced so I wouldn't be the one putting in all the effort. I took a step back. And if there was an instance where I wasn't doing my part in getting in touch with a friend, I would make a point of returning that call.

I had to cut back and get in balance. I wanted mutual relationships, not just relationships based on my planning and my calling and my effort. There was no pressure or expectation for others to return my call immediately. If they called a week later, that was okay. I would get around to calling them back when the time was convenient for me as well. There was freedom because I didn't expect anyone to call right back or feel slighted if they didn't. Life went on. My friends would call when they got a chance, and I would call them when I got a chance. I just needed to see things for what they were and be aware of the dynamics in my relationships. God was telling me I needed to pay more attention. I needed to make conscience decisions. I needed to make decisions based on reality not my perception. I needed to see who was really there for me.

A White coworker I had never talked with gave me a compliment on my skirt. I said thanks. She went on to talk to another White girl in the lounge where we were sitting. She was done with me. From past practice, I felt, she thought I would have continued to engage them in conversation or try to be included in what they were talking about. But, no! I said thank you, saw what was happening, picked up my book, and continued to read. I could spot the false inclusion which was the reason behind the comment. Certain people engage you initially only for you to pay attention to them. They are conditioned to believe if they engage you, you will continue to want to be included and salivate waiting on that inclusion.

They want you to chase after the inclusion. If you don't know for yourself what is going on, ask God for discernment. He gives it liberally. I pray for God to give me discernment so I will know in my heart what is real.

# HEALING

A White older guy was so surprised when I walked by him without speaking. It seems to me he jumped back. But mind you, he did not speak either. He just expected me to. I have freedom—if I choose to speak, okay; if not, okay. And the same with you. If you choose to speak to me, that is your choice. If not fine, life goes on.

An older Black guy did the same thing. He was so used to me speaking first that it took him by surprise when I didn't. He didn't speak. He just called my name, and I said "Yes?" People won't speak. They will just say your name, expecting you will react with "Hello." It's like getting your attention. By saying your name, it reminds you that you are in their presence and should be speaking to them. What a bunch of crock. Well, I am more aware and less reactionary and will say "Yes?" when my name is called, or I will call the person's name back. It's not about speaking. It's about responding to others instead of reacting.

You can check this behavior out for yourself. Don't speak first for a day or a week and watch the reaction of those around you. Speak only after someone speaks. And if someone engages you in conversation, just answer their question if you want to answer it and see what else they say to you. See if the conversation ends there or if they continue to talk to you. Another thing you should notice is how they react when one of their friends comes into the room. Do they completely turn their attention to the other person and dismiss your presence with no more eye contact, no more inclusion in the conversation? It's as if they talked to you because there was no one else to talk to, but when they have a choice, they don't choose you. This tells you what a person truly feels about you. Be aware of how you feel. Check out their nonverbal cues. I made it a point to stop being there for someone when talking to them was convenient for them. I will not make them a priority when I am an option.

What not speaking first does is show you who you are chasing. When you stop speaking first, you'll know if there is mutual respect in the relationships you have with other people. If so, they will take up the slack and speak first. If not, then they are expecting you to acknowledge them first. Ask yourself, "Why is that? Why is speaking first incumbent on me? Why do I have to work at the relationship with very little effort on the other person's part? Why am I chasing after them and trying to be included? Is it because of fear?" Do you feel you need them and can't live without them? Are they your idols, your gods? Ask the true and living God to reveal your idol gods and He will answer you.

We need to be aware of what we are doing and why. God wants us to lean and depend on Him. He is our source and our strength, not anyone else.

Watch other races. Do the Chinese make it a point to speak to other races? Do the Hispanics go around speaking to other races, or do they walk around as if they belong where they are and are not deterred by what other races think? We need to walk around with pride, with reliance on and in God and not in those we are trying to impress so they will include us in what they are doing. God wants us to connect with Him, more so than with anyone else. God wants us to fit in with Him. God wants us to turn and speak to Him.

The question to the mutual-respect-test is: Is there mutual respect in the relationship that allows you to not speak first and the other person picks up the slack because it doesn't matter who speaks first? They can speak just as easily as you did. Or do they look at you crazy because you aren't acknowledging them? How does it make you feel to not be acknowledging them? Work through those feelings. Ask yourself why you feel that way. Do you feel obligated to speak first? Why is that?

Do they not speak first now that you aren't speaking? Ask

yourself why. Why was it so easy and acceptable for you to speak first, but they weren't willing to? What does that say about the dynamics of the relationship? Who is chasing whom? Who refuses to? Is there balance?

Some people will say, "But I'm friendly. I like to speak." I am not saying don't speak. I am saying don't speak *first*. Pay attention to the way people respond to you when you don't speak first and they decide to. I noticed I would receive accusatory attitudes from people when they would speak. I would hear in their voices, "What do you mean not acknowledging me?" or "Did you not see me. Hello?? Acknowledge me." It's as if they wanted me to feel like saying, "Oh, hi, I didn't notice you, that's why I didn't say anything. I apologize."

I learned and practiced saying hi back with no fanfare, no guilt from overlooking them. No condemnation. I said a firm and simple hi with strength as if things were as they should be. There is nothing wrong with this picture. It's okay for you to acknowledge me and if not, that's okay, too, because speaking is your choice. It doesn't make me or break me if you recognize me or not. I want to know what I am really dealing with, what's in a person's heart.

This isn't about White people. This is about the Black race understanding that God is our way-maker and not anyone else. This is about you putting your trust in God and not in anyone else. This is about you seeing the people around you for who they are and how they actually feel about you. It's about you walking in God's strength and where He wants you to be, not below the standard He has set for you. This is about you realizing where your help comes from because what can a White person do for you that God can not do? This is about overcoming an inferiority complex. You can take pride in yourself because He has made you, not because of who you know or what you have or how you look, but because He is your Father and you are His child. That fact and belief will cause you to walk with your head up. Heads up!

I started to spend time at work by myself. Once I got use to the solitude, it was okay for me to be by myself there and in other circumstances. I went to the movies, lunch, Jubilee Theatre, walked with God, or I enjoyed my time at home with a good book. The more I did by myself, the more I was okay being by myself, and the freedom was awesome. I wasn't stuck at home missing out on life. I didn't have to have a man with me to go somewhere. I didn't have to have a girlfriend either. My life wasn't reliant on someone else's plans or timetable. I took God with me as my date. I would hold His hand as I headed out the door. He is my loving Father. I wasn't living with regrets. I was becoming independent. I was becoming God-reliant and less reliant on others.

I experienced a bad attitude from the lady who was working at the cleaners, so I said to myself, "I don't have to do business with you, and I can take my clothes and money somewhere else." I rode with my clothes in the car for about a month before I found a suitable cleaner. If the lady with the negative attitude doesn't want me in her store or my business, well, believe you me, I don't have to be in her store. Thank you, God, for the revelation. I don't have to put up with her rudeness and disrespect. If someone doesn't show me respect, I won't engage them. So if Tommy Hilfiger doesn't want me to wear his clothes, thank you for telling me. I have other choices; I can make my own clothes. He won't be getting my money. If I continue to do business with a disrespectful person, I am, in essence, saying his or her behavior is okay. I am condoning that disrespect by continuing to do business with those types of people.

I remember being at work and everyone gathered in my boss's office. Maybe he had called a meeting, but I hadn't been notified, so I remained in my cubicle doing my work. If he doesn't want me there, I don't feel slighted one bit like I used to feel. Have your meeting. I'm not going to invite myself or feel left out. If you want me there, you will let me know. Then what do you know? My boss would stop by my cubicle to see what I was doing since I wasn't trying to be included in what he was doing. I wasn't bent out of shape because I wasn't with them. I wasn't complaining because I felt out of the loop or didn't know what was going on. I was included in the most important loop, you see. No need to chase behind them. Got who? Got God, and He gives me what? That's right, *everything I need* in spite of others.

The more I wasn't trying to be included, the more people engaged me. I saw that some of the people who I had stopped speaking to first would purposefully not speak. They only spoke when they wanted something from me. They weren't my friends, nor did they have my best interest at heart. They just wanted to get information out of me. They would smile, get the information, and be gone. They would not talk to me again until they wanted to know something else. They were just being nosy and in my business. I set boundaries that told them to get out of my yard. That was no place for them. They were not invited. I let people in who I wanted in, and others were not welcomed because they were imposters anyway. It's powerful when you are the one being exclusive with someone. It's OK to say, "I don't want you in my circle."

I also wasn't making those who wanted me to elevate them feel special by acknowledging them and their presence. They were through with me. I wasn't bowing down. I wasn't doing a song and dance. I wasn't going along to get along. Not everybody liked Jesus, and He wasn't swayed. I wanted to be more like Him. I had taken my power back, and they didn't like my transformation one bit. Who cares? God was happy with me, and that's what matters.

To be excluded felt good. To exclude felt good. I was no longer allowing someone else to control me by saying if I didn't do this or act a certain way I wouldn't be included. Well, if I have to act like you want me to and not be myself, I don't want to be included. Get to steppin'. Got God, my strong tower and my provider. Got God, my way-maker and mind-regulator. Got God, my peacemaker. Got God, my redeemer and my rock. Don't need you or yours.

I realized I didn't have to say thank you for every little thing someone did. For instance, I was having lunch and when the waitress brought me my tea, my meal, or bill, one thank you for all those items would suffice. I don't owe anyone a thank-you for every little thing. The waitress was doing her job. When you overdo something, that's what it is, overdone. And how could I say thank you more times to a waiter or waitress than I had said to God that day and He had given me life, money, a car, and the means that allowed me to be having lunch? I needed to get my thank yous in order. God deserved them. It's okay to say thank you, but I give them at my discretion, not because people feel I owe them. I was not obligated.

I learned to trust a person after I had a reason to. Trust is something you build. It is not automatic. Why should I trust someone? When I initially meet a person, they don't have a proven track record with me. God said to renew your mind, work out your salvation with the renewing of your mind. Ephesians 4:21–23 says, "Surely you heard of him and were taught in him in accordance with the truth that is in Jesus. You were taught, with regard to your former way of life, to put off your old self, which is being corrupted by its deceitful desires; to be made new in the attitude of your minds."

Boy, I had a lot of mental working out to do, but I thank God for the process since I am a better person because of what I went through. My problem was I was too naïve. I thought most people were kind and loving, like I had seen growing up. What a wake-up call. I was taught to treat people like you wish to be treated, so if I was kind to them, they would be kind to me. Someone forgot to mention the part where you could have not done anything to someone and they would not like you and treat you badly. You could even be nice and kind, and they would still treat you badly. But with that I thank God because that person is just showing me who they are. Then I know what kind of person I'm dealing with.

I began to see who really cared about me. I even noticed a change in men. Men will speak to women first if we let them. Sometimes as women, we need to be quiet, mind our business, and let them come to us. And that's what I did. My smile was no longer automatic. Smile for what? Because you want me to? I got news for you. I don't react to you anymore. I respond. And if I choose to smile, it is my choice. God gave me joy on the inside. Now I am guarding my heart and not reacting but responding to the situation. Every smile from someone does not deserve a corresponding smile.

First Thessalonians 4:11–12 says, "Make it your ambition to lead a quiet life, to mind your own business and to work with your hands, just as we told you, so that your daily life may win the respect of outsiders and so that you will not be dependent on anybody."

Smiles can be deceptive. I was maturing from being so naïve. My question on my face was, "What do you want?" I decided to trust a person in time, with reason, but not right off the bat. No more of that.

Now that I wasn't making a big deal out of men but minding my business, I would notice when I was at the gym, the more I looked straight ahead, the more men would walk past me and try to get my attention. It was like a mating dance. First, the guy would stand off in the distance to catch my eye. When I didn't respond to that, he would walk by. When I didn't look his way, he would work his way to the machine next to me. It was so funny. I just kept my mind on what I was there for and let him do the dance. Often he would never say a word. It was all about the pursuit. He wanted to know how much effort it was going to take to get my attention or if getting my attention would be easy because I really desired that he would talk to me. If my posture said I was minding my business like the Word tells me to, it really intrigued him.

I often noticed out of my peripheral vision that men would just watch me. They were checking me out. It was nice to be the one being checked out instead of checking them out. I was putting things in order.

I realized the guys we date often engage us so we feel a connection, then we drop our guard only to have them withdraw from us, which makes us desire the connection with them again and chase after them to get it. People want you to validate them. They want you to feel they are important. No more. Thank you, Lord, for the insight.

When Charles and I first began dating, he mentioned going to the Taste of Chicago. I was so excited about the possibility of the trip, but nothing ever became of his suggestion. I got my hopes up for nothing. I don't know if he was planting a seed, hoping I would plan everything. I do believe now that's what he was doing, like so many guys. They will get you interested, to excite you, by suggesting the possibility of doing something, and then leave it up to you to make things happen. It's up to us to realize what they are doing, then we can say to ourselves, "He said 'maybe.' That also means 'maybe not.' He didn't make plans, just a suggestion." It helps to see things for how they are, which keeps us from getting frustrated. Maybe he was used to women doing all of the legwork. Well, I believe the man who God has for me will be one who can follow through with his plans.

Another time, Kirk and I were dating. I met Kirk after dating Charles, and he mentioned how he wanted us to go bike riding and fishing. These were the two things he knew I enjoyed doing. I listened to him talk, and I watched his actions. Nothing. It was as if he wanted me to be excited about the possibility, and then I would call him and pursue him, wondering when we were going to get together. Oh, no, brother. God opened my eyes to this behavior, the "maybe syndrome."

Gary called, and we went out a couple of times. He was a guy I met at Brooklyn's Jazz Café. I enjoyed his company. Then for whatever reason, he stopped calling. I noticed he hadn't called, but the fact that he didn't call didn't really matter because I was doing me. About a year later, out of nowhere, Gary called and wanted to get together. We met at a Starbucks and had an interesting conversation. A couple of months went by, and again, I didn't hear from Gary. It was the funniest thing. I was not going to chase him or any other man. They are free to go.

Sometimes I think these men wonder if the lady is dating, so they throw a feeler out to gauge. Sometimes I think they are having problems in their present relationship and want some additional company. Sometimes I think maybe they are just bored and want some company for the moment. Sometimes the man wants to play it cool and not seem anxious. He doesn't want women to think he is desperate. The main reason I believe they behave this way is because they want us to pursue them. They are saying with their behavior, "If you don't pursue me, then I'm not going to call you or come around. And then you are going to miss this prize possession."

So many men have been conditioned by the reactions of women. A man will mention plans and not follow through, which causes the woman to chase after him because the woman wants what he has suggested. Pavlov was a scientist famous for demonstrating that if you give a dog something to eat every time you ring a bell, soon the dog starts to salivate when you just ring the bell because it has associated one stimulus with the other. It's the same way with men. The ladies they date enjoy spending time with them, and after a while, they just offer to spend time with the women, who begin to salivate, wishing for the reward of being with these men.

Awareness of the situation is key. We have a choice to step back for a moment and witness what is happening. Is a man putting a carrot in front of his woman's face because he's so conditioned to seeing women chase after the *hope* of being with him? He wants her to chase after what he is offering or what he has. And if so, we can make a conscience choice to not chase that carrot. We accomplish this by not allowing their proposals to get us so excited that we plan everything or nag them about their suggestion. We don't run after what they are offering; we simply allow them to give to us. We can see the proposal for what it is—just a suggestion—and say, "Oh, well, maybe he will follow through but maybe not. We will see. I am not affected by what he does or doesn't do. I can make a conscious choice to not get bent out of shape if he doesn't follow through. His proposal doesn't make me or break me. His calling or not calling doesn't rock my world. His follow-through, or lack thereof, doesn't ruin my day. He doesn't have that kind of control over my feelings. He is not the be-all to end-all. If he doesn't make plans, life goes on. I am not thrown off one bit."

Now, *that's* girl power!

At the same time, you can see he is not a man of his word and you can let him know he is not a man of his word. Ecclesiastes 5:5 says, "It is better not to vow than to make a vow and not fulfill it." Men need to know that. It's up to us to tell them.

God gave me the revelation that men are no big deal. He is.

People want you to make a big deal of them. They want you to validate them and make them feel important and more special than they are. Tell that man with your actions, "You are no big deal, mister. I have replaced you with God. Where I once made a big deal of people and things, I have now changed my focus from you to God, and I make Him the Big Deal."

Some of our Black men have this bad. They think they are a hot commodity and women will do whatever it takes to get one of these rare creatures. Well, God showed me the importance of keeping my eyes on Him instead of the situation. I had to put my trust in the One who can give me a mate when there are one hundred women to one man because He is a way out of no way. He is a one-hundred-women-to-one-man God, one who can hook you up when the numbers look dismal. I trust Him, not the numbers. I trust Him, not men. James 1:16–18 lets us know, "Don't be deceived, my dear brothers [and sisters]. Every good and perfect gift is from above, coming down from the Father of the heavenly lights, who does not change like shifting shadows" (brackets added). God is a way-maker and will provide a spouse for me in His due time.

God wants us healed, but we must do our part in the healing process. What is God telling you to do? What book has He suggested for you to read by someone who has been through what you are going through, but you haven't found the time to read it? What classes has someone suggested you attend, but you come up with all the excuses in the world to not do so? How bad do you want to be healed? How much do you want to be better?

Is what you are doing in your relationships working for you? Do you desire a different outcome? Make time for your healing. John 5:6 says, "When Jesus saw him lying there and learned that he had been in this condition for a long time, he asked him, 'Do you want to get well?'" Now Jesus is asking you, "Do *you* want to get well?"

# 4

# The Problems

As I look back over my life, I want to capture the things I did that were outside of God's will for me so I can look at them, confess them, stop repeating those errors, and grow from the experience. Exodus 16:4–5 lets us know God tests us: "Then the Lord said to Moses, 'I will rain down bread from heaven for you. The people are to go out each day and gather enough for that day. In this way I will test them and see whether they will follow my instructions.'"

I wanted successful relationships. I knew I had to do my part to change what was happening in my life. Joshua 1:8 says, "Do not let this Book of the Law depart from your mouth; meditate on it day and night, so that you may be careful to do everything written in it. Then you will be prosperous and successful." I had to change what I was doing to make my relationships successful.

With my ex-husband, Antonio, our biggest issue was his verbal abuse. I allowed what he said to affect me because I wasn't secure in who I was. I was living below the standard God had set for me. Antonio's opinion was just that, an opinion, but I took what he said to heart, like his words were gospel.

Antonio would tell me I looked like a monster because I had

adult acne. He would tell me I had thunder thighs when my thighs started rubbing together. If I dropped something on the floor, he would scream that I wasn't paying attention. I remember once driving to Memphis for a funeral and leaving the cell phone charger in the rental car. When he found out, he tore me a new one. I had an accident in the car we had just purchased for him. He came out to inspect the damage but never asked if I was okay. In essence, he was telling me what my father had told me, that I couldn't do anything right.

We would be at church, and I would be singing, and Antonio would tell me I was singing off-key. He would tell me I was sweeping the floor wrong. Antonio would fuss about my driving. He would be belligerent. He would curse me out.

It seemed it was always something. Every day, all day.

Sometimes it would be a week before he let an issue go. I was relieved when he had to go to work and I had time at home by myself away from his condescending comments. He was accustomed to fussing because he had grown up in that environment. At times, I would get so tired of him that I would leave home.

But I kept going back. Antonio would promise he had changed and that he was sorry. Sometimes the change would last three months, sometimes six months, but in the end, he would revert to that same behavior. I know now I was choosing to go back to the same situation. I could have told him I was staying away until he got the professional help he needed. I could have said I would wait until he sought the assistance that would help him once and for all with his anger, and in time, we could consider reconciliation. Maybe that would have been the incentive that would have made a difference, because as long as he saw me coming back, nothing changed. I had to change my way of thinking about the situation and how I was dealing with it. The change started with me. I had to decide I would not continue to put myself in that situation.

The way to tell when you should go back is when that person is repentant. When we repent, we confess our sins, ask for forgiveness, and sin no more. There is evidence of repentance. Do not go back without the evidence of change or you can expect to get the same treatment. As I look back on my relationship, I realize Antonio stopped talking about my weight when I started telling him he looked like an Ethiopian with his big gut. He could give it, but he couldn't take it. However, I didn't want to live like that, criticizing my husband.

For my healing, I read God's Words about me, and I meditated on what God said about me. I allowed God to affirm me, and I began to understand that I am His child. I replaced Antonio's words with God's. God made me, and if anyone has a problem with the creation, he can take it up with the Creator, because I am fearfully and wonderfully made in God's image. I told myself this every day for as long as it took me to truly believe it. Ephesians 4:13–15 taught me not to be affected by what others said.

> ... until we all reach unity in the faith and in the knowledge of the Son of God and become mature, attaining to the whole measure of the fullness of Christ.
>
> Then we will no longer be infants, tossed back and forth by the waves, and blown here and there by every wind of teaching and by the cunning and craftiness of men in their deceitful scheming. Instead, speaking the truth in love, we will in all things grow up into him who is the Head, that is, Christ.

I have learned that it is my choice to believe or not to believe what others say about me. It is all just their opinion unless their words are true and edifying. What does God say about who I am and what I do? So who should I believe—them or God? Let me see. I put the media's opinion in one hand and God's opinion in the other. I put my boyfriend's opinion in one hand and God's opinion in the other. I put my father's opinion in one hand and God's opinion in another. For me, God's opinion outweighs everybody else's, and when I learned this vital lesson, it changed my life. I didn't always get it right. I would listen to what others said, but the more I practiced listening to God, the more I studied His Words, the more I mediated on His Words and took them with me, and the more I believed Him instead of anyone else, the more my confidence increased because I believed what God said about me.

God's Word was teaching me that I was chosen and royalty. First Peter 2:9  says, "But you are a chosen people, a royal priesthood, a holy nation, a people belonging to God, that you may declare the praises of him who called you out of darkness into his wonderful light." Now, *that's* good news.

You are special—unique—one of a kind—a gift from God! A person cannot make me feel a certain way unless I allow them to. Only if you give them permission to control you and your thinking do they have that power. If you say no, you choose to weigh what they say against what God says about you, then you retain control of your thinking.

So the next time your mate wants to tell you that you don't measure up, and his words are condemning and not edifying, remember *you have a choice* to believe him or not. He can think what he chooses, and you have a choice about what you think. Now if he is saying something that will better your life, then it would behoove you to listen. If you can't tell the difference, ask him why he says what he says and to show it to you in the Bible. It's in there if it's what God would have you to believe. By having him take you to God's Word, this will show him how judgmental and controlling he is in his thinking if his words do not line up with God's.

The second issue I experienced with Antonio for the first year or so in our new house, was that I did practically all of the housework. One day, I realized I was tired and didn't feel like I had had a weekend off from work. I started wondering why. Then I realized I had spent my entire weekend cleaning the house, grocery shopping, and cooking. We both had forty-hour-a-week jobs. It was then that I said I would ask him to help around the house. He was receptive to the idea, so we split the household chores. I understand that it is the wife's responsibility to be a worker at home and to maintain an orderly and organized home, but there is no reason we can't ask for help (Titus 2:5).

Antonio would get in the car drinking an alcoholic drink and want to drive. Now we would be in the house chilling all day and he wouldn't be drinking, but when we were getting on the road, he wanted to drink something. What I could have, and should have, said was, "I will drive if you drink, or I will stay home and you can go by yourself." I love choices.

Antonio was verbally abusive to his children when they would come and stay with us for the summer. I wish I had protected them more by telling him when he was being too harsh.

If I had known when I was married what I know now, I would still be married. Marriage isn't a bad thing. It's our ignorance of God's Word, God's way of handling the situation, and disobedience that get us into trouble. I was willing to learn a better way, and God was willing to teach me. I am sure things will go much better for me the next time around because I have learned some very important lessons.

After my marriage dissolved, I wasn't ready for a relationship. I needed some "me" time in order to learn the lessons God was trying to teach me from my marriage so I wouldn't be taking that baggage into my new relationships and making the same mistakes. I should have said no to dating someone so soon after my divorce.

We took things slow, Charles and I. We were three months into the relationship before we had sex, and I was still telling him no when he decided he was tired of hearing me say no. I should have never been in that predicament in the first place. We would be kissing, and he would perform oral sex on me. It was still sex. I should have said no to the oral sex. It's back to the conditioning. When a man asks you if he can perform oral sex on you, it's just another avenue to get you to have intercourse.

I'm sure Charles had never met a woman who was fine receiving oral sex for three months. I believe he was conditioned by other women's responses that vaginal sex came immediately after oral sex. That's what he was after. But I was different. I was old-fashioned, and while I was married, I could count on one hand the times my husband and I had oral sex. He was old-fashioned, too, and having sex "the standard way" worked for us. So when Charles brought on his talents with the oral sex, I was hooked. I hadn't experienced anything like it before. I didn't have to have it any other way. I would wonder to myself what he was doing because it felt so good. The man had mad skills.

The sex with my husband was good, but it wasn't earth-shattering, and I didn't have to have it. My response to the oral sex wasn't *"Let's have sex."* It was, *"This is so good I don't want to do anything else."* I was inexperienced and thinking, *What else could be this good? Nothing! So why mess things up with physical sex?* And then came the day we had physical sex. It was better than the oral sex. I couldn't believe it. He was trying to get me hooked with his marvelous lovemaking, and his plan worked because he had perfected his sexual skills. But I still wanted more. The relationship was dominated by sex.

Sex alone will never sustain a relationship. There has to be more ways of relating. I realize now that sex was his modus operandi to get the hook in. He wanted me hooked on his good sex so I would desire him above any other. *Knowledge is power.*

Initially, Charles used a rubber but said something about not being able to "feel" me and the rubber was not comfortable for him. I had already told him if we were going to have sex, he needed to take the HIV test and he did. I had seen the results, but there were other diseases, and I knew in my heart I should have said no to his request not to use a condom, but I allowed him to not use one—a big mistake. I should have said no, even though I was on the pill. What if he had syphilis or gonorrhea and had given it to me? I could not have blamed anyone but myself for my bad choice. By this time, I didn't want to lose him, and I said yes to his request out of fear of losing him and being by myself without a man.

I allowed Charles to call at inconvenient times—first thing in the morning, even on my off days. I thought he was being thoughtful, but now I think at times he was calling to make sure I was alone. He didn't want me doing what he was doing, or he could have been just thinking of me and wanted to say hi. Either way, I should be decent and in order. I must respect myself and ask the guy I am dating to call at a more convenient hour. I needed my rest. Plus, my mother taught me there's a time and place for everything under the sun. To tell him to call me at a better hour just lets him know I respect myself. First Corinthians 14:40 tells us, "Let all things be done decently and in order."

Charles would call after I had gone to bed and ask me to come over and get in the bed with him, and I went. I would put something over my pj's and head out. If I had been thinking, I would have at least said, "No, you come to my place." But at that time in my life, I wanted to be wanted, and I wanted to be with someone. After being married for ten years, it was hard sleeping by myself. I wanted companionship and a warm body. One day, my brother asked if I was Charles' booty call. I had never thought about it that way. *Never!* I know that is not what I wanted to be, so I gradually stopped going over at the last minute at that time of night. Thank God for my brother and his wisdom and him seeing the situation through a man's eyes. I was caught up and needed to hear the truth.

I would spend money on tickets to shows and plays for both of us. This was role reversal. There should be a balance. I would find myself purchasing most of the tickets. I wanted to go to different venues. If I want the man to be the man, I need to allow him to take the lead as the provider, as we will read about later in the biblical story of Jacob and Rachel and Boaz and Ruth. Instead of taking him, I could have taken a guy friend or girlfriend, but not the guy I was dating. My mother use to say, "Start off like you plan to finish," so I had to ask myself if this was what I wanted to continue doing. No, I wanted a man to provide if it is in his means to do so.

Charles came to expect this treatment and took me for granted. A woman is to allow a man to do for her what is in his heart to do, but sometimes, they can't because we are doing it all. Even if he chooses not to get the tickets, that's his choice, but the lady shouldn't make a habit of buying the tickets and taking the man. We can always go with a girlfriend or by ourselves. A man will come through if you mean something to him. He will move heaven and earth for you so take off the pants and give them back to him and be still and let him be the one who pursues you. The evidence of desire is pursuit.

I would also suggest to Charles that we go on weeklong vacations and weekend getaways. After my marriage, I had two timeshares and I was accustomed to vacationing with my ex-husband. I enjoyed visiting exotic places. Well, I wanted to go with my boyfriend, but I didn't see the damage I was causing our relationship by doing this. When you do everything with your boyfriend, there is no expectation for the future. There is no desire, no longing, no mystery, nothing new. You have done it all and seen it all. What's the point in getting married? I didn't see this then, but thank God for the lesson. I was living a married life, but I wasn't married. Now I take my weeklong vacations with my girlfriends or church groups for singles and when I become serious with a man, I will tell him only the man I am married to gets the privilege of accompanying me on vacation.

Charles would be thoughtful and want to pick something up for me when he was at the grocery store, but I wouldn't think of anything and would say I'm good. I was so accustomed to giving that it was hard for me to accept blessings. That was his way of taking care of me, and I didn't let him be the man he was designed to be. He would call me on his way to work and want to pick me up a breakfast sandwich or share his lunch, and I would ask, "Are you sure you have enough?" If the man wants to share, let him share. It's his job to know how much he has.

I had to stop trying to control the situation with Charles and let him give to me—say yes to the good. I don't want to be that old lady who says her husband never does anything nice for her. Well, when your man tried to bless you with something, you didn't let him, so stop complaining. We as women are so accustomed to being givers that we need to have a balance and be able to receive. The key is balance.

Charles told me when I was with him that I was never to open a door. I didn't understand that him getting the door was his display of chivalry. He was providing and taking care of me. I didn't understand how important it was to allow him to do those things. Now I know to let him do for me what he wants and accept his kindness and generosity. We women often have that I-can-do-it-myself mentality, and we end up cutting off our own blessings. Renew your mind and allow your man to comfort you, allow him to protect and provide for you. You desire the provision and protection, but if you continue to tell him no, when the time comes that you want him to take care of you, he will refuse since you told him no so many times in the past. It's all about accepting the good that he does.

Women are such nurturers, sometimes we need to be the nurturee. Let God bless you through others. Stop telling God no to His blessings. He is blessing us through the men in our lives when they provide for us.

# 5

# What I Learned From Each Relationship

I mention the things I learned in each relationship because it is an exercise to see the good. No relationship is all bad. These people were in my life for a reason. Remembering what I learned from each person gives me a truer perspective of my relationship with that person and what they added to my life. Everyone in my life is a teacher. I can learn something from them if I open myself up to the lesson. It may be what to do; it may be what not to do.

## ANTONIO TAUGHT ME:

To know what kind of relationship the man has with his mother before you decide to marry him. This is vital because he will treat you like he treats his mother. Antonio fussed with his mother. They argued often. Their relationship was tumultuous. I had never seen anything like it, and after I married him, I said somebody should have told me that a man will treat you like he treats his mother. Now I tell you so you will know and consider their relationship.

    Pay attention to his behavior when he gets mad, because this shows you his problem-solving skills—or lack thereof.

Pay attention to how he acts when you disagree with him. It will let you know if he will try to control your thoughts or if he can respect your opinion. Antonio didn't want to hear what I had to say. It was as if he thought God hadn't given me a mind to think for myself. *What in the world?* It seemed he wanted me to accept his train of thought, and he would continue his stance until I was just tired of hearing it. There came a time in our marriage that I decided I could not talk to him, so why try? I didn't want him to always agree with me. I wanted us to be able to agree to disagree and for him to realize I had an opinion just like he did and he could take from it what would bless him. But no, it had to be *his* way or else. There was no reasoning with him.

Antonio had the personality of my father which helped me to see that the significant relationships of your youth will often dictate the character of the person you attract unless you deal with the hurt of those relationships—or lack of relationship—by confessing the hurt, forgiving that person by praying for them, and allowing God to heal you. Some examples are: If your father was not in the picture, how is that affecting your relationships? If you were molested growing up, how is that showing up in your relationships? If one of your parents was on drugs or domineering, how has that affected your views on relationships? Nehemiah 9:2 says, "Those of Israelite descent had separated themselves from all foreigners. They stood in their places and confessed their sins and the wickedness of their fathers." We should pray that God will forgive the wickedness of our fathers.

I learned that when Antonio would call me names like monster or thunder thighs, this was his insecurities showing up. Misery loves company, and only people who are insecure or immature make degrading comments about someone else. His derogatory comments show what kind of person he is more so than defining who I am.

I can't fix someone. When I met Antonio, he was hurt because his wife had left him and taken his kids. I had felt his pain and wanted to make things better for him, but what I ended up doing was jumping into some mess. He had issues he had not dealt with, and no matter what I did, I could not help him. He had to help himself. He needed to realize what happened to him in his last relationship happened to him for a reason, and it was up to him to grow from the experience. I ended up being a cushion for him, and he didn't get a chance to self-evaluate. Now I will ask a guy what he learned from his last relationship and if he could do things over, what would he change. If he didn't learn something, he is bound to repeat the lesson, only this time, you will be a part of the equation.

I was judgmental when it came to choosing a mate. There is nothing wrong with having an idea of what you want in a mate, but remember, God may have a different plan. He sees the big picture. I had said I didn't want to marry a police officer or a man with children. I never wanted children for myself. I ended up marrying a correctional officer with the federal prison system who had two small children. I didn't want the baby momma drama, but God had other plans. The relationship was better between me and his ex-wife than between the two of them. The kids were a blessing in disguise. We would go swimming, to the park, bike riding, to the movies—all the things I enjoyed doing, I was able to do with them. I almost missed my blessing, thinking I knew what was best for me.

I have learned to pray about a matter with my mate and let God guide our hearts. One time Antonio and I were arguing and I said to him, "Let's pray about it." We did and that prayer stopped the argument dead in its tracks. The prayer had worked, but for some insane reason, I never mentioned praying again during an argument.

## CHARLES TAUGHT ME:

One of the first things Charles said to me when we started dating was for me not to change. It wasn't until years later that I knew what he was talking about. Charles had dated his share of women. He had seen women change from being independent initially to dependent on him. He had come to realize that spending too much time with a woman made the relationship become old real fast. Charles was telling me in essence he had dated women where he saw them every day or close to it. He talked to them too often. He spent too much time with them, and the relationship had gotten old real quick. He didn't use those words, but now that I know the man, he was telling me not to change from the person I was when we first met. Who I was initially is what attracted him, not the woman I would become.

He wanted to continue to be interested in the woman he met, not some metamorphosis that took place mid-dating. He admired me because I had hobbies. He liked the idea that I volunteered. He appreciated the fact that I had friends and did things with them and wasn't asking him to spend all of his waking moments with me. He enjoyed the fact that I gave him his space. He appreciated my independence. Ladies, men need their space, and if we don't give it to them, they will take it.

In those demanding relationships where women superimpose themselves into a man's space without being invited, he will disappear to slow things down. He will disappear to get some breathing room. Charles didn't want to move too fast. He had experienced that in the past, and it had always ended where he or the woman felt spent and "too" familiar. He wanted the relationship to last, so he would purposefully slow it down.

As women, we often see this pulling back as an insult. We think they are engaged in someone else when more often than not, they want to slow the relationship down, not get too used to you, and not get too familiar too soon. Familiarity breeds contempt. When we don't pull back, men end up pulling back. They are declaring that they have had enough. What woman wants a man to say, "I have had enough of you? Can I get a break?" Not me!

So we must realize men will play it cool. In the beginning, they'll be rational as opposed to emotional. They don't want to seem weak by being too desperate. No man wants to be perceived as weak, so what do they do? They pull back. They apply the brakes.

Other times, men pull back deliberately to see what your reaction will be because they are curious to see if you are desperate. They want to know how you will respond to his disappearing act. If you put up a big fuss because of their absence, men have you right where they want you. Women, we tell men by our reaction how much their absence affected us. Did his absence have you bent out of shape and upset? If so, why is that? What did you tell him by your reaction? *Oh, I have her right where I want her. She isn't going anywhere. She can't live without me. Watch this. All I have to do is go without calling her for a few days and she is hysterical.*

You don't want any man thinking that. You want him to know you have a life that doesn't revolve around him. Your life is not controlled by his whereabouts. It isn't on hold because he hasn't called. He's doing his thing, and you are doing yours.

Charles would want me to think he had other options with women, even when he didn't. He would exaggerate. He did this to make himself look more attractive to me. My friend Greg did the same thing. He would tell me about all of the hot women he had dated. He wanted me to think, *He's the man!*

*Whatever!* If these women were so hot, why wasn't he with those beautiful, fine, sexy women he was telling me about? And if these women have it going on like that, why was he calling and coming to see me? It's a ploy. Men may consider your physical appearance, but it takes something deeper than just looks to keep him. Ladies, we must go deeper, deeper spiritually and mentally. Song of Songs 8:10 says, "I am a wall, and my breasts are like towers. Thus I have become in his eyes like one bringing contentment." The words, "I am a wall," say I am secure in who I am. I am stable and sure of myself. "My breasts are like towers" illustrate my maturity. Being secure in who I am and mature brings contentment to the man I am dating.

Men use other women to make us jealous all the time. They want us to think they have choices and are hot stuff. All that matters is how a man treats you. Just pay attention to them. I have noticed that a man will deliberately talk to a lady in front of me because he wants to get my attention. He is talking to her but looking at me. He wants to see my reaction. It's conditioning. Men are so conditioned to believe a woman will find them more attractive if some other woman has them until they use that tactic quite often to make us jealous. Be smart.

Charles would flirt with other women to check and see if I would be insecure. I thought it was rude and very bad behavior, and I told him so. This just shows us how much power we have over them. They want to make us jealous. Why would men want to make women jealous? Because they want to increase their worth! They want to appear more desirable. They want us to think, *I could lose him to another woman so I had better work harder to keep him.*

When we see this behavior, we can smile to ourselves and say, "How cute. He's trying to make me jealous. He must really like me to put in all that work. If he wanted to be with her, he would be. He chose me." All we have to do is realize what is happening, put a smile on our face, and walk away. That will blow his mind and say with our actions, "I see what you are doing, and it's not going to work."

Actions speak louder than words. Try it. What walking away says is that you can live with him or without him. Walking away lets him know what God has for me is for me and I'm not afraid of you looking at her. The next time you catch your man looking at another woman, let something else capture your attention. When he doesn't have your attention, he will try to regain it. This is one key to relationships. Whenever your man isn't giving you some attention, let something else capture yours. He will wonder where you went. He will come looking for you. I am talking about positive things, not something that would damage your relationship. I like to allow something in my surroundings catch my attention. It may be something in my purse, a store window, or even picking at my nails. It might be a painting, a flower, or the texture of a piece of wood. I might just look up and admire the sky. If you are in a store, go look at a dress. If you are in the car, pick up your cell phone and call someone. Do anything that takes the attention off him.

Men want attention. Why do you think they purchase Hummers and live in the city? Do you think they plan to pull someone out of a ditch with it? Why do men go to the gym and get big muscles? Do you think they need them for their jobs? I don't think so. They are trying to get our attention. And if their muscles or cars are what attract us, that shows what kind of people we are. We must look at a person's spirit, not their possessions. How does he treat you? How does he treat others? First Samuel 16:7 says, "But the Lord said to Samuel, 'Do not consider his appearance or his height, for I have rejected him. The Lord does not look at the things man looks at. Man looks at the outward appearance, but the Lord looks at the heart.'"

Charles taught me to hide money somewhere in my car so if I'm ever out and need some cash for food or gas or whatever and I don't have my purse, I will have some money in the car. He also taught me to wipe my butt really good after a bowel movement. If you don't wipe from the rooter to the tooter, you may have a stinky booty. He would use baby wipes.

Have good boundaries. If Charles didn't want to go somewhere, he wouldn't go. I wanted him to go with me furniture shopping. He said no. If he didn't want to eat something or go somewhere, he would say no to my request. I might ask again, and he might change his mind or he might not, because he didn't live in the frustration of going and doing things that he really didn't want to do. I now adore that about him. I say "now" because I have learned that behavior for myself. God doesn't tell us yes to our every request. I learned to say no, and I learned to respect Charles' no as well. He has the freedom to tell me no and with that, I have the freedom of choice to go with someone else or by myself. Giving him his freedom and exercising my choices are beautiful things.

He also set up ground rules from the beginning of our relationship, that there was to be no hitting, no name-calling, no arguing in public.

Wear the right size shoe. For years I claimed I wore a size eight shoe and my feet would hurt. He said to me one day that I should try a half size larger. I did, and my feet have been fine ever since.

Focus while driving. I would eat, talk on the phone, read, and reach for items on the backseat. Charles told me to concentrate on the road—if not for me, for the safety of the people around me.

Take vitamins.

Do resistance training to build muscle, which increases

metabolism, which burns more calories. I was fearful of looking like a man, but my muscles really look good on me because I look toned. And I would rather have muscle instead of fat any day.

Eat less carbohydrates (i.e., white bread, sugar, white potatoes, pasta, rice) because what I don't work off during the day turns into fat that is stored around my waist and thighs. Instead, I eat more vegetables, fruit, grain, seeds, nuts, and meat.

Have a life. While dating Charles, I noticed that when I was busy with friends and hanging out and doing my thing, he was interested in me and where I was and who I was with and what I was doing. As soon as I didn't have anything planned with anyone and was waiting to see what he and I were going to do, he became indecisive about getting together. For example, when we first started dating, I was attending a book club and would get with the girls to do different things. He would want to come over just to give me a kiss and be on his way, but he wanted to be where I was. I volunteered with Big Brothers Big Sisters and Meals on Wheels. Once, I took him on a Meals on Wheels run. He got excited about delivering the meals with me and helping others. I think it also excited him to see me committed to something of value and importance.

When I was out with friends, he would call and call trying to get in touch with me. When I was living my life, he was interested in me and what I was doing. When I kept my appointments and schedules with my friends, he would call. He was in hot pursuit. When someone else had my attention, he wanted it, but as soon as I made less time for others and more time for him, he seemed to stop by less often and his calls came less frequent. I noticed a pattern. When he would pull away, I would say to myself, "Okay, I will give you your space. They can have you." I started hanging out with my friends again. Eventually he would feel my absence and come around.

# MY TESTIMONY

What I learned from this whole experience is to keep my life. There needs to be balance. I spend some time with him but not all of my time. I should not make him my life. That's important because we both need time together and time apart. Balance makes for a healthy relationship. We all know too much of anything isn't good for us. And being in the company of a man too much only makes him desire you less because you are always there. Give him a chance to miss you and want to be with you.

I remember Charles would mention to me that some girl at the gym tried to get his phone number. I would see him watching other women's butts as they passed by. He would flirt with the waitress who was taking our order. He would even mention women on TV and ask me which one I thought was the cutest. At the time, I didn't pay him any attention, but in hindsight, I realize he was trying to make me jealous. Men will test you to see how secure you are.

There came a time when he would see a beautiful lady and just stare at her. I finally realized what he was doing, and I would excuse myself from his presence so he could get a good look. I would be gone about twenty-five minutes. When I got back, I had his complete attention. I gave him the freedom to stare all he wanted. He had the freedom to get her number if he chose to. I want a man who wants me. I don't want to be with someone who wants someone else.

Any man is free to leave and pursue his soul mate. I would never interfere with that. And I don't have to be jealous of another woman or fight to keep a man. If you want someone, set them free by saying with your actions, "You are free to go." If they were meant to be yours, they will come back, but if you force them to be with you, you only end up pushing them away. Give them the freedom to choose you, because you want to exercise your freedom of choice.

# WHAT I LEARNED FROM EACH RELATIONSHIP

A man will tell you everything you need to know about himself. Often Charles would share things about himself, but I wanted to talk about me. I had to learn some listening skills and learn to be quiet and let him share and be tuned in to what he was saying. He was telling me everything I needed to know. I just needed to listen.

Give people a chance. Initially, I didn't think Charles was my type. He was popular and handsome and had been a jock in college. *Not my type.* Those kinds of men seem stuck on themselves, stuck with muscle power and no brain power. How completely wrong I was in my perception. Charles was one of the most intelligent men I had ever met. He was thoughtful and caring. Go figure. And if I had not given us a chance because I was being judgmental, I would have never gotten to know what a caring, kind, thoughtful person he could be. I have since learned to give a person a chance. It behooves me to get to know that person instead of making a judgment call.

Men will test you. Charles would say he didn't like my blouse or fingernail polish color. I stopped wearing the blouse and changed my fingernail polish color. Looking back, I should have said, "So what? I'm okay with it." Since I had gone through a verbally abusive marriage and was broken, I wasn't sure what was appropriate and acceptable. I now know I needed to renew my mind and get my dating values and standards set so I would know what I would and would not accept. Being in a vulnerable state, I accepted behavior that normally I would never have.

Charles was so busy trying to not be caught by some woman he failed to realize I wasn't chasing him. I just wanted to be with someone who wanted the same things I wanted, so if a man didn't want to be with me, "Later gator, after while, crocodile." Charles was accustomed to women chasing him. He was used to women trying to make him their husband and the father of their children. He was running. I was not chasing. I loved him enough to let him go. I loved me enough to let him go.

But I wasn't honest about my feelings with Charles. His bad behavior would hurt my feelings. I would suck it up and distance myself instead of dealing with the issue. I would not talk to him about what was going on with me. I should have been honest. After asking myself why something hurt my feelings and getting some understanding, I should have talked to him about it, at least once. Although there were times I felt he did things on purpose to hurt my feelings, I could have told him about it, then if his behavior continued, I would have realized he was showing me what kind of person he was. He was showing me his character, and it was up to me to live with his behavior or not.

And if I accepted his behavior, I could only blame myself for that choice. At the same time, I had to ask myself why his actions had hurt my feelings. Why did he have that kind of control over how I felt? When I chose to stop reacting to what he was doing but to respond with wise choices, I was able to take control of me. When a man's behavior does not produce the desired result he was hoping for, we take our power back.

Charles mentioned us going to his family's home for Christmas dinner but didn't call on Christmas to let me know if we were going. Then there was the time he said I could drive his Hummer on my birthday, but when my birthday came, he didn't mention giving it to me. I didn't confront his behavior and lack of follow-through. I just let it go. He didn't have a clue how I felt about his lack of follow-through, because I didn't tell him. I complained about it to everyone but him. I had learned in my marriage to not talk about a matter with my spouse, because it didn't do any good.

Well, Charles was not Antonio, and I owed it to him to discuss what I was upset about. Sometimes we assume a person should know why we are upset and realize that their behavior is hurting us, but if we don't tell them, we are saying that we are okay with their behavior, because we haven't said otherwise. First Corinthians 2:11 tells us, "For who among men knows the thoughts of a man except the man's spirit within him?" and Matthew 18:15 says, "If your brother sins against you, go and show him his fault, just between the two of you." I had to learn to address my issues and not run from them.

## KIRK TAUGHT ME:

Men will test you to see how far you will go and how far you will let them go, but if you tell them "No" to their nonsense, they will respect you for respecting yourself. Kirk would want to come over after he got off from work at 11:00 P.M. He worked for the post office. I told him no way. Sister was going to bed. He would tell me he wasn't used to a woman not asking him to come over to be with her. He would call me, and I would say I was busy. It would blow his mind. He was like, *What? She isn't dying to be with me?* He would tell me he wasn't used to dating an independent woman. He liked my independence.

Men will try to make you insecure. There was a time when we were sitting in my apartment looking at the cover of an *Essence* magazine and Tyler Perry and the beautiful actresses of his latest movie were on the cover. Kirk commented on how beautiful one of the women was. I mentioned how sexy Tyler Perry's lips were, how juicy and kissable they were, and that was the end of his comments. Men can dish it, but they can't take it.

## WHAT I LEARNED ABOUT ME:

"You and I are essentially infinite choice-makers. In every moment of our existence, we have access to infinite choices. Some of them are made consciously, while others are made unconsciously." To live our best lives "... we should become consciously aware of the choices we make in every moment. Whether you like it or not, everything that is happening at this moment is a result of the choices you've made in the past. Unfortunately, a lot of us make choices unconsciously, and, therefore, we don't think they are choices, yet, they are."[1] Haggai 1:5 says, "Now this is what the Lord Almighty says: 'Give careful thought to your ways.'"

"... most of us—even though we are infinite choice makers— have become bundles of conditioned reflexes that are constantly being triggered by people and circumstances into predictable outcomes of behavior. "[1]

For instance, if my man is with me and chooses to speak to a woman, I have the choice to be jealous. I do not have to respond the way he intends for me to. I don't have to be predictable. If my man doesn't call for a few days, I have the choice to be anxious or I can choose not to allow his behavior to upset me.

The Bible shows us how God provoked the Israelites to jealousy by putting the Gentiles in their place. Romans 11:11 (KJV) shows us, "I say then, Have they stumbled that they should fall? God forbid: but rather through their fall salvation is come unto the Gentiles, for to provoke them to jealousy." Men do the same thing. They say with their behavior, "You see, she is getting what you should have."

How do we not become jealous or anxious? I'm glad you asked. First, we keep our eyes on our Father and His promises for us instead of what the man is doing. Jeremiah 29:11 tells us, "'For I know the plans I have for you,' declares the Lord, 'plans to prosper you and not to harm you, plans to give you hope and a future.'" If

---

1    *From the book The Seven Spiritual Laws of Success © 1994, Deepak Chopra. Reprinted by permission of Amber-Allen Publishing, Inc. P.O. Box 6657, San Rafael, CA 94903. All rights reserved.*

# WHAT I LEARNED FROM EACH RELATIONSHIP

God wants a certain man in my life, that man will call. If not, God will put up a roadblock that will keep him from getting in touch.

Second, we understand that in each instance we are making a choice. We are to do what God instructed us to do: we give careful thought to our ways and how we are allowing other people to affect us.

Even if we get jealous or anxious, upset or lonely, we don't have to stay stuck there. We feel what we feel and then we remember God's promise in John 14:27 (KJV): "Peace I leave with you, my peace I give unto you: not as the world giveth, give I unto you. Let not your heart be troubled, neither let it be afraid." We have a choice on how we feel and how we respond to others.

I am a giver. I need balance in all my relationships. The lesson God showed me in my relationship with men transcended to my other relationships. He said, "balance." God showed me I was a giver with my ex-husband and with Charles. I was also a giver with my family and friends. I was such a giver I found it hard to receive. I found it hard to allow people in my life to bless me. I wanted to be the one who was giving. I wanted to take care of people and make their lives better.

God showed me where I had been saying "No" to allowing Him to bless me through others. God showed me I needed to give and be able to receive as well. Jesus allowed Mary to wash His feet, so it would behoove me to allow others to bless me by giving to me and helping me. Receiving blessings allowed me to feel rested, restored, and cared for.

So if the new man in my life wants to pick something up from the store for me because he is thinking about me, I am going to think of something I want or need and allow him to bless me. Even when my brother came to pick me up from the airport when I went to visit him and his family, I would give him money for gas. I was always picking up the check when the family went out to dinner. I would pay for the movies, the aquarium, practically everything. My brother loves me and wanted to bless me, so I stopped being the one who paid for everything.

I had a girlfriend come stay with me when she was in between places. She offered me some money after she had moved out. The old me would not have accepted the money. I would have justified not taking it by saying I was helping her. But I learned it's okay for me to help her and it's okay for me to receive a blessing from her. Say "Yes" to the good. I accepted the money.

In both of my relationships, the men pursued me. Antonio saw me out one night when I was with friends, minding my own business, not even looking for a date, and asked me for my number. Charles was very determined to spend time with me even though I told him "No" to intercourse for three months. This spoke volumes to me. If a man wants you, he will make the moves it takes to have you.

Maturity is a process. I try to improve and learn something every day. I don't get down on myself for long when I mess up. I forgive myself, and I am forever thanking God for the lessons and loving me enough to show me a better way to handle situations. The better way is His way.

I am more aware of myself now. If I get depressed or am feeling low, praise CDs always give me a boost. There is something about praise and worship that takes away the sadness, but when I am in my bed and feeling alone, I allow my tears to flow and I tell God all about it. I say, "Father, I want a mate. I want someone I can feel. I want someone's arms around me. I want someone who will help me build Your kingdom." I remind Him that He sent the disciples out in twos. And this confession puts a smile on my face and in my heart because He knows all about what I am going through and will bless me in His time. I just needed to get what I was feeling off my chest.

# WHAT I LEARNED FROM EACH RELATIONSHIP

There is something therapeutic in telling God all about it. It's like I'm not denying my feelings but living in truth, and He meets me at my needs when I do this. He becomes my rock, my shield, and my provider. He lets me know I have Him and I am not facing this trial of loneliness by myself. He didn't say we wouldn't feel lonely. He said He would see us through our loneliness.

I was so busy complaining about Antonio's verbal abuse that I didn't appreciate his goodness. I also didn't take the time to understand what was causing his anger. I just saw what it was doing to me and shut down. We did go to counseling, but knowing what I know now about how your childhood affects you until you deal with it, I would be more inclined to talk to him about why he did the things he did. Now, I take a look at the fruit of a person and the root of a person. I should have shown more grace by understanding what was behind the behavior. Instead, all I did was look at how it was affecting me. In truth, it wasn't all about me. The arguing was what he knew. It was what he had been exposed to.

If I want to be more like Jesus, who looked beyond my faults and saw my needs, I will look past what my mate is saying to the pain that is causing it. I would ask the guy I am dating why he behaves the way he does, if he has asked God to help him deal with the issues of his past, if he has forgiven those who hurt him by praying for them, if he asked for forgiveness for the sins he has committed, if he has forgiven himself, and if he has decided to walk in the light of obedience. It is a process that works, but you have to try it for yourself.

I pray for the people God puts in my life. I pray for my enemies. Who knows the last time someone put their name on God's altar to petition the Lord for His intervention on that person's behalf? I pray for them because I know prayer changes things. I may not be able to help them, but I know who can.

# MY TESTIMONY

I pray for understanding, wisdom, and discernment.

Sometimes when I share with people what I have been through, they want to use my past mistakes to put me down, but I don't let them because I have grown from the experiences and I thank God for the growth. Don't let someone label you by your past behaviors and mistakes. Know that you are a work in progress and there is no condemnation for those who love the Lord.

Previously, I didn't accept feedback or criticism very well. I learned to open myself up to what people were saying and compare it to what God was saying so I could grow. Everyone and every situation can teach me something. I started asking, "Lord, what am I to learn through these people and this situation You have put in my life?"

When I was growing up, I had an uncle who had diabetes. Doctors had to cut off his legs. I didn't want anyone cutting off my body parts. I learned all I could about the disease and how to avoid it. I learned from my uncle's mistake. We are to be watchful and learn from the mistakes of others.

I became tired of thinking about Charles. It was two years after we had broken up, and he was still on my mind. I had dated Kirk, but I thought about Charles and our experiences so often I would get mad at myself. I would say, "Lord, I want to move on and get over him. Why do I still think about him so much?" It was like the more I tried to get him off my mind, the deeper the thoughts sunk in. I was pissed. I wanted him out of my head and out of my heart so I could move on, but there were reasons I couldn't get him out of my mind. One, I had to realize how much he had meant to me. Two, I had to realize it takes time to get over someone. Three, I realized he may always have a place in my heart because of our experiences and that was okay. The truth set me free. Admitting I still had feelings for him released me to live in truth. It was at that moment I was able to smile when I thought of him and be at peace.

John 8:31–32 says, "To the Jews who had believed him, Jesus said, 'If you hold to my teaching, you are really my disciples. Then you will know the truth, and the truth will set you free.'"

I want someone who brings out the best in me. I desire a relationship where the person will tell me the truth without being condescending. I want a relationship where I can make a mistake and not be condemned. I want a man who is growing and willing to teach me so we can grow together. I want a relationship where my God-given rights to have an opinion are respected. I want collaboration not competition, a relationship where we are building each other up not tearing each other down.

I learned I was in a vulnerable state after my divorce. I overlooked some things about Charles' character that if I had been whole, I would not have overlooked. I accepted disrespect that, had I been whole, I would have dealt with differently. The same goes for Antonio. I saw his derogatory way of communicating, but I chose to overlook it. Be careful to be aware of what behavior you may be overlooking about the person you are dating because of your brokenness.

I realized by not having sex with my companion, I am able to get to know the person for who he is and my thoughts aren't clouded by how I feel about the intercourse. By abstaining from sex, I won't fall in love with what the man did to me but with the actual person. Dating within God's limits allows me to learn how to relate to my companion while delaying sexual expression. Dating done correctly teaches self-control and delay of gratification. I want to know that my spouse has self-control. I want to have self-control. It's a good practice to tell yourself "No" sometimes. I realized by not having sex, I was able to leave a bad situation much easier than if I had shared my body with a man.

As I have grown and I talk to people about coming into the light, I can't expect them to understand the life I am living for Christ. They are still in darkness. I remember I was once there, and I am to be patient and continue to plant seeds that someone else will water. God gives the increase.

Charles would talk about his girlfriends. They were "just friends" is what he said. He would mention how they would hang out or how they would do things for him. This didn't bother me because I had guy friends who could one day become his friends and vice versa. I wasn't insecure about that. Who but an insecure person doesn't want you to have friends of the opposite sex? But he never introduced me to his so-called female friends, and we dated for two-and-a-half years. After a while, I started to think, *Something is wrong with this picture.* If they were truly just friends, what was the problem with me meeting them?

I had a guy friend when Antonio and I lived in Memphis. He got to know Antonio, and they became such good friends that he was in our wedding. Evil loves darkness; the truth loves light. I had nothing to hide and didn't mind them getting to know each other.

I rarely told the man in my life how much I appreciated the good he had done. God wants us to make it a point of being appreciative. When we give praise for something a man has done that is noble, it is easier for him to listen to us when we confront him about a mistake. We are to build our men up and let them know when they have done a job well. This also allows us to have a true picture of our relationships. We aren't just concentrating on what he does not do. We see and acknowledge all he does that is excellent and praiseworthy. This gives us a truer prospective of our relationship so it is not plagued with complaints.

After having sex with Charles and Kirk, the intensity of the pursuit diminished. Things definitely changed after we had sex. After having sex, it seemed instead of wanting to date, they both wanted to have sex.

I learned men will say whatever it takes to get you to do what it is they want you to do. We should listen to what men say, and we should pay attention to their actions. They are telling us all they want us to know about their feelings through their actions. Love is an action word. It is realized, not just spoken. It materializes into something tangible. For God so loved the world that He gave …

You may want to ask, "What do you do to show me you care for me?" I say this because a man's way of showing you may differ from your way of showing him. God made us different. The point I'm trying to make is if a man cares for you, he will show you, not just tell you. There will be evidence of how he feels about you. Ask yourself, "What do I see?" not "What do I feel?" Often, feelings are how you want things to be and how you perceive them.

I learned what my issues were because God named them. He told me what I was dealing with so I could participate in the healing process. He brought my issues into the light so I could be aware of them. You can't deal with something until you are made aware of what you are dealing with. This way, too, I can guard against these issues when they try to rear their ugly heads in the future. Awareness is key.

Listen to the Holy Spirit. Charles had said "No" to going to many places with me after I told him about my plans. I would tell myself I was through asking him to go because it seemed he always said "No." Well, I would be talking to him, telling him my plans, and the Holy Spirit would tell me not to invite him, because he wasn't going to go. The Holy Spirit told me that Charles was going to disappoint me yet again. Now mind you, Charles would tell me he didn't have anything going on, and because of that statement, I felt obligated to invite him. I would ask him if he wanted to go in spite of what the Holy Spirit had said, just for him to say "Maybe," but not follow through again. I just kept hoping he would go. I wanted him to. The Holy Spirit was telling me all along not to ask him. I would ask again instead of obeying God. All I can say is, I did it my way and there was frustration and disappointment as a result. I should have listened and obeyed the Holy Spirit.

The Holy Spirit tells us what to do so things will go well with us. Do we want distress in our lives or things to go well? Deuteronomy 5:29 says, "Oh, that their hearts would be inclined to fear me and keep all my commands always, so that it might go well with them and their children forever!"

I had to work through my hurt. The relationship with Charles really hurt me. And I, in turn, treated Kirk like crap. It was all misplaced, undealt with anger. Anger is never to control us. Ephesians 4:26–28 teaches us, "In your anger, do not sin: Do not let the sun go down while you are still angry, and do not give the devil a foothold. He who has been stealing must steal no longer, but must work, doing something useful with his own hands, that he may have something to share with those in need."

Because I had allowed the anger to stay within, because I had not acted in faith and dealt with it in God's way, my anger was destroying my relationship with Kirk. It was the reason for my violent outbursts. For that reason, Jesus tells us in Matthew 5:22, "But I tell you that anyone who is angry with his brother will be subject to judgment." Anger that simmers within is like committing murder in your heart because it is rearing its ugly head in your actions. It's okay to be angry and have your feelings. Just don't stay stuck by letting the anger control you. Give your anger to God.

Some man may have abused you, and your anger is justified. Your anger may be righteous anger, but if your soul is going to be right within you, if you are going to have peace in your life, then you must forgive and believe, and as it says in Romans 8:28–29, all things will work together for your good in order to make you more like Jesus.

## WHAT I LEARNED FROM EACH RELATIONSHIP

Are you being controlled by your anger? Give your anger to Him. The guilty will not go unpunished. Our righteous God will come to your defense and vindicate you in His time and His way. Therefore, like it says in Ephesians 4:31–32 (KJV), "Let all bitterness, and wrath, and anger, and clamour, and evil speaking, be put away from you, with all malice. And be ye kind to one another, tenderhearted, forgiving each other, just as God for Christ's sake hath forgiven you."

## GOD WANTS TO TEACH US:

Looking back on my life, I realized my ex-husband was on the rebound when I met him. He was not divorced from his wife yet. He hadn't sorted through his last relationship in order to grow, change, and be a better person. He was bringing those same issues into our relationship. Here are some questions I will pay attention to regarding the next person I date in order to understand where they have come from and where they are going, which is the root and fruit of a person.

"Where have you come from?" (Genesis 16:8a) That was the question the angel of the Lord asked Hagar when he met her as she was running away from her situation with Abram and Sarai. Hagar was quick to tell the angel of the misery she endured at the hand of Sarai, but she failed to tell him that her attitude and behavior were some of the reasons causing her current situation. We play a major role in why we are in the situations we experience. It helps when we examine ourselves.

"And where are you going?" (Genesis 16:8b) The angel wanted to know if Hagar had any direction for her life. Something had been wrong in her past relationship. Hagar replied she was running away from her mistress. The angel of the Lord told her to go back. Why would the angel of the Lord tell us to go back to the relationship we just left? There is a reason we were in that relationship in the first place. There are some things about ourselves that we need to change.

Going back to a previous relationship may not always be a physical return. It is often a mental return. It is a time of reflection and examination. What about your behavior and standards, or lack of standards, caused things to turn out like they did?

People come into our lives to show us ourselves, the real us—we aren't trying to deal with— behind the mask. The people we attract are often a mirror of ourselves since we refuse to look in the mirror and self-examine. What we don't like in others is often the same things we refuse to see in ourselves. They are just our reflection.

Even when opposites attract, they are there to show us our shortcomings and areas where we could use some growth. What we grumble and complain about in others are often our own issues. Romans 2:1 explains, "You, therefore, have no excuse, you who pass judgment on someone else, for at whatever point you judge the other, you are condemning yourself, because you who pass judgment do the same things."

Now it's *your* turn. Write down everything you have learned about relationships from your past and present experiences. Write down causes and effects. Write down what you learned about yourself. Ask God to help you self-examine and be your guide. You may have learned you call the man you are interested in too often and he ends up taking you for granted. You may have noticed when you didn't answer your phone, for whatever reason, he would keep calling to get in touch with you. Maybe you were too controlling. Maybe you were a nagger. Write it down. Ask God to shine the light from heaven on your soul.

# 6

# My Frustrations

I had to revisit my previous relationships to understand what I was running from and had not dealt with. I had to examine what had happened that caused me to be in that predicament in the first place. I had to mentally go back and examine what behavior needed to change. Where did I need to submit to God's teachings?

I remember going to Houston with Charles and he would look at every woman in the jazz club before he decided to pay me any real attention. In hindsight, I believe Charles was lusting after these women. I was his main squeeze, but he was always on the prowl for his next notch. I remember he would look and decide there was no one in the place worthy enough for him to pursue, then he would turn his attention to me. He could have been looking to see if he could spot one of his old girlfriends, one of his present girlfriends, or his next challenge. I don't know. (This is what I felt was going on anyway.)

I remember during that same trip we went to dinner with his friends and he left and went to the bathroom when the bill came. I took his credit card and paid the bill. He was so pissed that on the way home, he called some other woman while I was in the car with him. I held my hand out for him to hold as we drove down the highway, and he just looked at it. I felt like I was three inches tall. He just totally disregarded me. I realize now that he was mad at what I had done, and instead of addressing the issue with me, he was punishing me to show me how upset he was. He was revengeful. It was okay that he was upset. I'm sure I did a lot of things he didn't like, but we never dealt with what was bothering him. He would just put distance between us instead of talking his dislikes over with me.

Idols always demand sacrifices. When someone fails to satisfy our demands and expectations, our idol demands that he should suffer. Whether deliberately or unconsciously, we will find ways to hurt or punish people so that they will give in to our desires. This punishment can take many forms. Sometimes we react in overt anger, lashing out with hurtful words to inflict pain on those who failed to meet our expectations. When we do so, we are essentially placing others on the altar of our idol and sacrificing them, not with pagan knives, but with the sharp, cutting edge of our tongues. Only when they give in to our desire and give us what we want will we stop inflicting pain upon them.

We punish those who don't bow to our idols in numerous other ways as well. Sending subtle unpleasant signs over a long period of time is an age-old method of inflicting punishment. We see this when a person has the attitude, "Get in line with what I want or you will suffer." There is opposition to free will. Such behavior is an act of unbelief. Instead of relying on God's means of grace to sanctify the person, he depends on his own tools of punishment to manipulate others into change. By being perpetually critical, he can make people miserable until they give in to his idols. The usual result of such behavior is a superficial relationship.

As James 4:1–3 teaches, inflicting pain on others is one of

the surest signs that an idol is ruling our hearts. When we catch ourselves punishing others in any way, whether deliberately and overtly or unconsciously and subtly, it is a warning that something other than God is ruling our hearts.

There was a time when Charles and I went to Florida for a conference and we were in class. I had been thoughtful and put a Snickers bar in his man-purse. When he felt it, he said to himself, "What has this bitch done now?"

Then there were times when I talked to him while he was at work. Instead of saying he was busy and he would call me later, he would just rudely hang up the phone in my face. Then on Mother's Day, the year after my mother had passed, he called and said, "Oh, I'm sorry. I dialed the wrong number."

What a butt hole, but he couldn't do anything to me unless I let him. I had just been so hurt in my marriage that I considered this behavior "normal." I hate to say it, but I had become accustomed to dysfunction. Then there was the time when I called him, some woman answered the phone, then hung up after I asked to speak to him. There was another time when he told me his phone wasn't working and he didn't always get my calls or my messages. Thank God by this time I said to myself that it didn't make sense for me to call him since his phone wasn't working.

Sister just wanted to be loved. God wanted to mature me, heal me, and make me whole. He wanted me to go through this roller-coaster romance so I could understand what others have been through. Everything for His glory. He knew I wouldn't mind sharing in order to bless someone else. He knew I would say "Yes", I will tell my testimony of how I was in darkness and God brought me into His marvelous light and I have never been happier. What Satan meant for evil, God meant for good, and I praise Him.

Then at the end of the relationship, we would have sex, and he wouldn't even kiss a sister. Man, what a situation to be in! But God had a plan for all of what I had been through in this relationship.

I, in turn, did what Charles had done to me to Kirk. I wanted to know if what Charles had done to me would work on someone else. Dating Kirk was an experiment to see if I could get him to behave like all those women Charles had told me about.

When Charles and I first started dating, he told me how he had several of the prettiest, finest, most intelligent women outside his house in his bushes looking through his window and calling him nonstop trying to see what he was up to. So I wondered if what Charles had done to me, I could do to someone and have him behaving like those women.

So with Kirk, I would mention how I wasn't ready to be in a serious relationship and I didn't want to put a title on the relationship we had. I would tell him about the men I would meet and how they would call and come by. Once, I invited him to dinner and he said "No," so I took another guy friend and told Kirk about it the next day. It was the noncommittal-jealous-tactic in full swing. I learned this from Charles. I remembered how Charles' behavior had left me wanting more of him and I saw how I could do that same thing to the person I was dating. The less I wanted to see Kirk, the more he wanted to see me. I used all Charles' tactics on Kirk.

One day, Kirk called to see if I wanted to go out with him. I told him "No," that I had plans. When I walked to my car, I saw Kirk in my parking lot. *What the world?* Kirk had pulled a drive-by just like the women did that Charles had dated. I just want my sisters to be aware of this process. I believe men use the noncommittal-jealous-tactic to get us to respond to them in an insecure manner. *Knowledge is power.*

I never really felt Kirk was the one. He was just something to do until something better came along.

# MY FRUSTRATIONS

Know the signs, ladies, that perhaps you are his interim—just something to do until the love of his life comes. He doesn't want to be alone, so he dates you. This behavior is disrespectful and shows a lack of care about your feelings. He does just enough to keep you but nothing more.

I was on the rebound when I dated Kirk. One sure sign that a person is on the rebound is that they compare what is going on in the new relationship with what happened in their last one. I talked about Charles constantly. I talked about how good the sex was, about places we had gone, and moments we had shared. I criticized Kirk's old car, his old clothes, and his poor performance in the bedroom. I criticized him when he ate his asparagus with his fingers. He couldn't do anything right. Everything about him was wrong. It was obvious I had not let my past go.

A frustration I had when I dated Charles was that I would ask him to go with me to an upcoming event. I would ask him on Monday, and the event would be scheduled for the following Saturday evening. He would say, "Let me think about it." I had no problem with his desire to think about going. The problem was that by 4:00 P.M. on Saturday—the day of the event—I still had no idea what he was going to do for an event that started at 6:00 P.M. It was a very frustrating situation.

I realize now I was not in control of my life. I was waiting to hear back from Charles instead of exercising my choices. What I could—and should—have done was simply say to Charles, "Let me know Thursday by 7:00 P.M. if you are going to be able to go." That way, if he called by seven, I would know if he was going. If so, fine; if not, I still had a chance to make alternate plans. There is no guesswork or worry or being anxious from not knowing. (We live and learn, don't we?)

I could have said, "I would like to know by Thursday. If I don't hear from you by Thursday, I will just make alternate plans." What freedom it would have been to know if he was going to follow through, and if not, I still had sufficient time to make other plans. That would have been me taking control of my life. My life is my responsibility, not his. If I don't set limits, then he is in control. When I set limits, I am in control of me and what happens to me. I couldn't change him. I could only change my behavior and exercise my choices.

Charles would initiate plans and say he "might" want to go out on the weekend, and then I wouldn't hear from him. The weekend would come, and he never mentioned the plans. I was left hanging and frustrated. When the man you are dating states he "might" want to do something on a weekend, have him RSVP. So I will say, "Let me know by Wednesday if you want to get together." By asking him to let me know what the plans are, I am able to know in time if we are getting together. There is not guessing or worrying or being anxious from not knowing. Now I am learning to take control over my life instead of giving that control away.

Have your man call when he is leaving his house and on his way over to pick you up. This way, you know when he is on his way and you can finish getting dressed. And if he has not shown up in a reasonable amount of time, you can assume he is not coming, which gives you choices:

- You can call him and see what the holdup is.
- You can go on without him.
- You can go somewhere else you want to go.
- You can take off your clothes and decide not to go because of his lateness.

You teach a person how to treat you. If you don't tell and show the guy you're dating that his behavior is unacceptable, he will think it is okay when he blows you off.

There would be times when Charles would make plans and not show up. I remember once when he asked me to go and spend Christmas with his family. I had said yes. He said he would let me know how he felt after he got off work that Christmas morning around seven. I had already been invited to a Christmas dinner with friends and would not cancel with them because something told me in my spirit this event with him wasn't going to happen. He had not followed through with plans so many times before. Honestly, he hadn't said "Yes" or "No." He had said he would "let me know" once he got off. At 5:00 P.M. on Christmas Day, I got a text message from him asking how I was. I wanted to call him back, but my spirit had me calm down and text him instead.

By this time, I had read some books on taking control of my life, and I knew to consider what the person had shown me in their behavior, so I expected him not to follow through. I had seen his ways. I was not going to be fooled again. God didn't change the situation. He changed *me* in the situation. I executed my plan. I woke up around eight Christmas morning and cleaned my place. Dinner with my friends was at noon, so at 10:00 A.M., I showered and dressed and was out of the house by 11:00 A.M. Charles didn't call me, and I didn't call him. By now, I was just fed up and tired of his games.

Had I understood about choices and boundaries from the beginning of the relationship, things would have gone better for me. But all things happen for a reason, and I thank God for the lessons and the growth. I needed to go through these changes so I could write my experiences down to share with each of you in order for God's purpose to be fulfilled.

I had options. I had choices. I was not going to chase him down after he had asked me to go to Christmas dinner with him. No, if he wanted me to go, he would have called me, so his inaction was my answer, and if he had called after I left, oh, well, too bad for him. I had gone on and maybe next time, he would call me earlier, like he said he would. I had a wonderful Christmas with my friends. And when I texted him back, I said to tell everyone hello. I thought he had gone home without me. I wasn't mad, hurt, or upset. I was having the time of my life where I was. I would have been upset had I not gotten up and been sharing Christmas with friends because I was waiting on him, like I had done so often in the past. Growth is a beautiful thing.

Often we pray for God to change the other person. Well, God didn't change the situation or Charles; He changed me from being a victim to being victorious in the situation.

When a guy asks me out, in order that I know what to expect, I ask:

- *What do you have in mind?* This allows him to take the lead.
- He might say, "When do you want to get together?" I will respond, *"Give a sister some options."* This puts the ball back in his court.
- *What time can I expect you to pick me up?* If he is more than thirty minutes late, I can exercise my choices of going with him or not.

Kirk and I went to church together. Often he would be late. I didn't care to be late, so I called him one Sunday morning to see what time he was going to pick me up. He was still asleep. I told him I was going to drive myself and get there on time because that meant a lot to me. The next Sunday, he beat me getting ready.

Once when we were going to a concert in Dallas, I told Kirk what time I wanted to leave so we wouldn't be late, and, of course, he wasn't ready. I told him I was driving myself because I had my ticket and he had his. He couldn't believe I would not wait for him. I told him I would see him there, no problem.

Men will test us to see how we will handle a situation. They want to know if we will stand up for ourselves or fall for the "okey doke." They want to know if you will do anything and everything to keep them because you fear being by yourself or losing them. When we put our trust in God, who deserves it, we know God will supply our every need—not a man. Then we can let the man be free to live his life, and we can respect his boundaries and choices.

On another occasion, Gary invited me to his house. He was cooking dinner. The time was set for 7:00 P.M. I arrived at seven and rung the doorbell. No answer. I waited about twenty seconds and rung again. No answer. On my way back to my car, I called him. He answered and said he was on his way to the door. I waited in my car for about thirty seconds then took off. I went back home.

I was on I-20 when he called and asked where I was. I told him what happened and that I was on my way home. He said he had fallen asleep. With a smile, I told him to go back to sleep because evidently he needed his rest. He begged me to come back. I said "No, maybe some other time." He asked if we could meet at a restaurant. I said "No, get some rest." I was so happy with myself. I was not frustrated. I had taken control of me and not kept knocking or calling. I gave him reasonable time to answer the door, and he wasn't responding so I made a choice for myself. I chose to leave and keep my respect and dignity by not hounding him.

I can see how we women let men get under our skin. I could have been knocking and calling for a minute. I realize he could have had some other woman in his house, trying to make her jealous by having me come by at the same time she was there, and if I kept knocking and calling, it would have made him look like hot stuff to her. Or just the opposite, he could have had me inside and some other woman knocking, wondering why he wasn't coming to the door when she saw my car outside. We have got to stop *reacting* to men's behavior and instead, *respond* with the sense God has given us. By leaving, I was showing Gary my world did not revolve around him. He was not the be-all to end-all. They like to think that we can't live without them.

One Sunday, Kirk called me around 5:00 P.M., wanting to know if I would go to a Bruce Bruce comedy show with him that evening. I said "No, I had plans," and I did. My girls were over, and we were going out together. I didn't let him know that. That was none of his business. I stayed calm, I stayed kind, but I stuck with my "No" even though I wanted to see Bruce Bruce. I had learned to be a woman of my word with my friends. They are counting on me. I found out later that I was his Plan B. His original date had cancelled on him. I don't want to be anyone's backup. That's what we usually are when a man calls out of the blue with last-minute plans.

He doesn't value your time, because he feels you don't have a life or will drop whatever you are doing to be with him. So why should he plan and respect your time? By keeping my previous commitments, it showed him my life did not revolve around him.

I took my break-up frustrations out on Kirk. Kirk had his issues, and as I've said before, I treated him badly. The one thing I regretted and later had to apologize to him for, through tears, was for being so mean and cruel to him. He definitely got the wrath of my breakup and lost love with Charles. I even slapped him hard once, and would hit him hard all the time. It was crazy. And something inside me would say, "Would *you* want someone to treat you like that?"

I dealt with that inside my head, knowing I was wrong and that you reap what you sow. I definitely didn't want to turn into a mean, hateful person, because that is not who I am. And I didn't want him hitting me, so I figured that I had better stop. I prayed to God to help me with my anger, to not let me take my anger out on this guy, and to help me because I didn't want to be a mean person. I also asked my Father to help me get over the hurt, which I felt was the cause of this anger.

I hated Charles, but I knew it was a sin to hate so I tried to understand my feelings. Then I realized I didn't hate Charles. I hated the thought that my love was not realized. I hated that our relationship didn't turn out the way I had hoped and wished. I hated that I had experienced another failed relationship that had been painful, but I didn't hate Charles. I hated what I had gone through those restless nights. I had been so knotted up and stressed out over that relationship that I had to get massages to release the tension. When I stopped seeing him, the tension left. It was like a load lifted off my shoulders, and that load lifted every time I broke up with him.

I was just fearful of being by myself. I didn't want to be by myself. I missed the companionship I had in my marriage. I didn't have family in Texas, and my friends were cool, but I wanted a male companion, and I felt I put up with Charles' bad behavior just to have that male relationship.

Looking back, what was missing in my life was a trusting relationship with my Heavenly Father. In my singleness, I should have been cultivating a relationship with Him. God in His goodness wanted to change my restless, peaceless, joyless existence into one of peace, joy, and love. Hebrews 4:14–16 states,

> Therefore, since we have a great high priest who has gone through the heavens, Jesus the Son of God, let us hold firmly to the faith we profess. For we do not have a high priest who is unable to sympathize with our weaknesses, but we have one who has been tempted in every way, just as we

are—yet was without sin. Let us then approach the throne of grace with confidence, so that we may receive mercy and find grace to help us in our time of need.

I had even thought about getting revenge on Charles by putting raw scallops around his house. He would have had to move out once those scallops began to rot. But God said you reap what you sow. That behavior will come back on you. The ditch you dig for him will be your own. Romans 12:19 (KJV) says, "Dearly beloved, avenge not yourselves, but rather give place unto wrath: for it is written, vengeance is mine; I will repay, saith the Lord."

So I decided not to. To not hate him and be able to move on, I accepted my role in the situation. I took responsibility for the way my life had been. I accepted the choices I had made, which were why I was in this situation in the first place. There were curses in my life because of my sins. No sin goes unpunished. I had been getting a good whooping. God's wrath was upon me to get me to see the error of my ways. *I see, Lord, I see!*

I did not blame Charles and act like a victim. I learned the lesson and would not be stuck in a cycle. I had to reinvent myself and renew my mind with a new way of thinking and behaving. Doing the same thing was going to result in the same outcome. I had to change me so things would be better in my life.

I had to ask Charles, Kirk, and Antonio to forgive me. God told me to. It was part of the healing process. I had to take responsibility for the consequences of my behavior. Now I wouldn't carry baggage in my new relationship. I wouldn't have bitterness. I would grow.

I prayed for Charles. For thirty days, I prayed for him. All I can say is prayer changes things. Now I look at our experience in a whole new light.

# 7

# What Are Boundaries?

A boundary is a property line. Just as a physical fence marks where your yard ends and your neighbor's begins, a personal boundary distinguishes your emotional or personal property from what belongs to someone else. You can't see your own boundary, however, you can tell it's there when someone crosses it. When another person tries to control you, tries to get too close to you, or asks you to do something you don't think is right, you should feel some sense of protest. Your boundary has been crossed.

## THE FUNCTIONS OF BOUNDARIES

Boundaries serve two important functions. First, they define us. Boundaries show what we are and are not; what we agree and disagree with; what we love and hate. God has many clear boundaries. He loves the world (John 3:16); He loves cheerful givers (Second Corinthians 9:7); He hates haughty eyes and a lying tongue (Proverbs 6:16–17).

As people made in His image, we also are to be honest and truthful about what we are and are not. Dating goes much better when you are defined. When you are clear about your values, preferences, and morals, you solve many problems before they start.

The second function of boundaries is that they protect us. Boundaries keep good things in and bad things out. When we don't have clear limits, we can expose ourselves to unhealthy and destructive influences and people. Prudent people see danger and hide from it, but the simple keep going and suffer for it (Proverbs 27:12).

Boundaries protect by letting others know what you will and will not tolerate.

## WHAT'S WITHIN MY BOUNDARIES?

I remember Charles was thoughtful and would give me things. If he had a laptop, he wanted me to have one. When he got a Palm Pilot, he bought me one for Christmas. He brought me a poncho one day. He would give me vitamins and instruct me on taking minerals to ward off colds. He would give me information on detoxifying my body by drinking water and sweating. He would get me rain caps for my hair.

Eventually there came a time when I started to *expect* things from him. If he had something new, I wanted to know where mine was. He was already considerate and giving to me what he wanted to give, and that was a lot. It was wrong for me to nag him and pressure him to get me what he had gotten for himself. I like to give freely and not grudgingly. It was okay for me to ask and okay for him to say "Yes" or "No." I should have never demanded anything of him—and then be mad because he didn't deliver. How would I feel if he demanded something from me? I see now where I was trying to control his actions. I was crossing his boundary.

## WHAT ARE BOUNDARIES

When I started dating Kirk, I realized how I had made Charles feel. When I went shopping, Kirk would ask—and sometimes demand—that I buy him something because other women had. I told him if I wanted to buy him something, I would. He kept nagging me about purchasing him something. I told him he could not control how I spent my money, especially when he hadn't bought me anything but was looking for something from me. He wasn't even doing what he was asking me to do. What in the world was he thinking? Kirk was crossing my boundary.

To avoid these scenarios, we need to look at what falls within our boundaries and see what we are responsible for.

## FEELINGS

God has given us our feelings. I have heard parents tell their sons, "Boys don't cry." Did they forget that Jesus wept? I have heard a mother tell her daughter to "suck it up." In essence, the mother was telling her daughter that her feelings weren't valued. Our feelings are our responsibility. Oftentimes, our feelings cause us to do good.

Our feelings can also be what motivate us to harm others. There are many times when a person might seek revenge because of hurt feelings. We are to consider our feelings but not let them control us and what we do. We are taught, in spite of our feelings, to do what is right. God *will* hold us accountable, regardless of how we feel (Matthew 5:43–48).

Feelings come from your heart and can tell you the state of your relationships. They can tell you if things are going well or if there is a problem. If you feel close and loving, things are probably going well. If you feel angry, you have a problem that needs to be addressed. The point is, your feelings are your responsibility and you must own them and see them as your problem so you can begin to find an answer to whatever issue they are pointing toward.

I remember Antonio would call me "thunder thighs," and I took what he said to heart. I was five-five and no heavier than 130 pounds, but he still called me thunder thighs. When we would go out for dinner, before we would leave the restaurant, I would head to the bathroom and regurgitate my food. At home, I kept a knife or spoon in the bathroom so as soon as I finished eating, I would head to the bathroom and make myself throw up.

Now understand that Antonio called me thunder thighs because he wanted to and that's how he felt, but I had a choice to feel like I had thunder thighs or not, and if I did have thunder thighs, I could be okay with myself. By throwing my food up, I had allowed his feelings to become mine. He was controlling how I felt about myself. His words were affecting me because I was allowing them to. At any time, I could have said, "I am okay with these thunder thighs. You can take them or leave them."

People make comments about you and want you to feel bad about yourself. They only win when you say, "Okay, I believe what you say." We must realize God has given us a mind to think for ourselves, and we need to listen to the conversations that go on in our heads to make sure they line up with the Word. Sometimes we have very self-defeating conversations about ourselves going on inside us. We need to become aware of these self-destructive comments and replace them with biblical truths. We have to take control of our feelings and start loving who we are in spite of what others say.

Once, Charles went to Florida for job training for about a month. We were discussing who would pick up his mail during that time. He said he had a girlfriend who was going to get his mail for him. Now me being the helpful one, I wanted to do it for him, but he had made his choice. I could have felt slighted. I think I did for a hot second, but I shortly realized it was *his* mail and he could get whoever he wanted to pick it up. I choose to be okay with his decision instead of having hurt feelings.

I would ask Charles to go to church with me. After he said "No" a couple of times, I stopped asking. Then one Sunday while talking, he mentioned he had gone to another church. I thought, *Well, why didn't he go with me?* I was perturbed. I thought, *Why would he go to another church when he knew I wanted him to go with me?* I could have been upset, but soon I realized it was his choice where he went to church. At least he went! I couldn't control where the man went to church, and I couldn't force him to go with me.

I didn't want to struggle in this relationship like I had in my marriage. Antonio and I argued so much then. I wanted peace. I had argued enough for the rest of my life. I would own my feelings and work through them, and I would try not to control others and what they did with their life and time. I would not want someone to control me. This was truly liberating once I came to that realization.

There were times when my feelings would tell me "Enough is enough!" and to get out of the relationship. Our feelings are there to guide us, warn us, and protect us.

As women, sometimes we don't do what's right because we think doing what's right might hurt someone's feelings. We need to be aware and try to do what's right based on *God's* value system. It might hurt the guy's feelings that I am dating when I tell him "No" to sex. Oh, well ... It might hurt his feelings when I tell him he can't come over after 8:00 P.M. It might hurt his feelings if I don't give up my other male friends for him. It might hurt his feelings if I don't buy something for him when I go to the mall. It might hurt his feelings that I don't cook for him. Ultimately, *he* is responsible for his feelings. Did I sin against him by doing or not doing something?

## MY TESTIMONY

We need to understand it is okay for men to get frustrated when we are doing what is right in the sight of God. It is okay when we don't allow their feelings to control us and what we do. Hopefully, that frustration will help them seek a better way—God's way.

## ATTITUDES AND BELIEFS

Attitudes have to do with your orientation toward something—the stance you take toward others, God, life, work, and relationships. Beliefs are anything that you accept as true. Often, we do not see an attitude or belief as the source of discomfort in our life. We blame other people, as did our first parents, Adam and Eve. We need to own our attitudes and convictions because they fall within our property line. We are the ones who feel their effect, and the only ones who can change them.

The Bible has many examples of people not receiving what God had desired them to have because of their attitude. When the spies were sent to view the land of milk and honey, the land God wanted to give the Israelites, only two of the spies had the right mind-set and only those two were permitted to partake in the richness of God's plan. The others were sent to wander in the desert, never taking hold of the goodness that could have been theirs (Deuteronomy 1:19–36).

We must constantly check our attitudes and ask if God would be pleased with our outlook. When we believe something other than what the Word of God has set for us, we experience distress in our lives. We must establish our belief system so that it lines up with God's standard if we want to reap the benefits of peace, harmony, and goodness (First Kings 11:9–11). We must remember we are responsible for our attitudes and beliefs, and the actions we take and the consequences we face.

## WHAT ARE BOUNDARIES

I attended the Desperate for Jesus conference at Oak Cliff Bible Fellowship Church in Dallas, Texas, where Beth Moore, a renowned author, was the speaker. Through her words about my body being a temple of the living God, my attitude and belief about premarital sex changed. Now I realize that it is better to do it God's way so that I will not sin against Him. I became abstinent while dating Kirk, who would say to me, "We are going to get married anyway, so it's okay for us to have sex."

I responded, "No, I'm not having sex again before I am married." It didn't matter what he said or what he did or how frustrated he got. My attitude and belief toward fornication had changed. I was steadfast, unmovable, and abiding in the work of the Lord (First Corinthians 15:58, KJV).

My new attitude upset him, but he was responsible for his feelings, and I was okay with him being upset. I would rather he be upset than God.

## BEHAVIORS

Behaviors have consequences. As Paul says in Galatians 6:7–8, "A man reaps what he sows." If we show ourselves friendly, we gain friends; if we are obedient, we live in peace. Problems arise when we interfere with nature's design of sowing and reaping in another's life. If someone is a bad manager of money, the consequences he or she reaps should teach that person that what he is doing is wrong. But if someone steps in and prevents the consequences from happening, that irresponsible person seldom learns better spending habits. To rescue people from the natural consequences of their behavior is to render them powerless.

Women do this when they allow a man who is not working to live with them. Second Thessalonians 3:10 says, "For even when we were with you, this we commanded you, that if any would not work, neither should he eat." We prevent that man from taking responsibility for his life and suffering the consequences for his irresponsible behavior. Therefore, he stays stuck in an immature stance. There are no consequences for his idleness, and she is to blame.

We may give money or loan money to a person who has out-of-control spending habits. To help a person is not to keep them ignorant. If they want our help, we can suggest a money-management class or allow the natural consequences to teach them the lesson the hard way.

## CHOICES

We need to take responsibility for our choices. This leads to the fruit of self-control (Galatians 5:23). A common boundary problem is disowning our choices and trying to lay the responsibility for them on someone else. Often we might say someone "made us" do something and *they* are responsible for making us do what we did, as did our first parents when Adam blamed Eve and Eve blamed the serpent. This stance betrays our basic illusion that we are not active agents in many of our dealings. We think someone else is in control, thus, relieving us of our basic responsibility.

We need to realize we are in control of our choices, no matter how we feel. This helps us to make choices that are right for our lives. As God has from the beginning, He still holds everyone responsible for the choices they make. We receive blessings for obedience and curses for disobedience, but the choice is ours (Deuteronomy 11:26–28).

Throughout the Scriptures, people are reminded of their choices and asked to take responsibility for them. Like Paul says in Romans

8:13, "If we choose to live by the Spirit, we will live; if we choose to follow our sinful nature, we will die." Often, we have been so conditioned on what we should do for others that we feel obligated to do things God has *not* assigned us to do. Matthew 25:7–9 says, "Then all the virgins woke up and trimmed their lamps. The foolish ones said to the wise, 'Give us some of your oil; our lamps are going out. No, they replied, there may not be enough for both us and you. Instead, go to those who sell oil and buy some for yourselves.'"

These wise virgins are our example of our choice to allow others to be responsible for themselves. Often we feel an obligation to do for others when, in fact, the Bible teaches us to allow them to be responsible for themselves, which helps them to grow and mature. When we set boundaries, we are taking responsibility for our choices and the lives we live because of those choices. *We* may be the one who is keeping ourselves from being happy because of *our* poor choices.

It was my choice to have sex outside of wedlock and sin against God, and I had to accept the curses for my choices. God's Word tells me in Deuteronomy 11:26–28, "See, I am setting before you today a blessing and a curse—the blessing if you obey the commands of the Lord your God that I am giving you today; the curse if you disobey the commands of the Lord your God and turn from the way that I command you today by following other gods, which you have not known."

Once, a girlfriend told me how she had helped a male friend write his book. The more she helped, the more he asked her to do. Once the book was published and he was on tour, he never thanked her nor did he mention her in the book. He just used her, and she was resentful, but it had been her choice to help. At any time, she could have said, *"No, that's enough."* Will you say that with me? "No, that's enough." Very good. She had to take responsibility for her choices. He had not forced her to do anything.

## VALUES

What we value is what we love and assign importance to. Often we do not take responsibility for what we value. We are caught up in valuing the approval of men, rather than the approval of God. John 12:42–43 (KJV) says, "Nevertheless among the chief rulers also many believed on him; but because of the Pharisees they did not confess him, lest they should be put out of the synagogue: for they loved the praise of men more than the praise of God."

When we value what others say about us over what God's Word has told us, we miss out on life. When we live in fear of what others think, that fear keeps us from our full potential. We have essentially given our power over to the one whose opinion controls what we do. We literally bow down to their will, making them our god. Boundaries help us not to deny but to own our erroneous values so God can change them.

When I asked God to help me, He explained He had given me this love and passion, but I was not applying my focus to the people He had intended for me to. He told me to get another little sister with Big Brothers and Big Sisters, since my other one had grown up and she had a busy life, so I didn't see her as often as I once had.

Volunteering was my passion and was very important to me, and as I showed my new little sister and her family love, I realized more and more love in my life. Now I wasn't chasing a man to get love from him, or feeling unfulfilled because I wasn't in a dating relationship. God directed me to the place where I could give and receive love. Love was all around me, but I was valuing the wrong things. I had valued being in a dating relationship to the point that I was consumed by the desire to be dating and on my way to being married. I now valued my new relationships.

During my journey, God showed me how I valued what people thought. I would wear my best to work so I would be thought of highly by my coworkers. I would speak to people who didn't care about me in hopes they would accept me. God showed me why I did what I did. Then I began to value what He thought. After I got my thinking straight, I stopped wearing uncomfortable clothes and shoes, I quit trying to impress others, and I went without makeup and jewelry.

It felt so good to be liberated from the concerns of what others thought. It felt good to impress God, because He was impressed with my heart and my behavior, not with what I drove or wore or how I styled my hair. The experience was liberating. I stopped trying to impress people who didn't give a red cent in the first place. I stopped focusing on the external me—the way I looked—and started to focus on the internal me—my spirit.

## LIMITS

God is the ultimate limit-setter, and we would do good to follow His example. God does not set limits on others; He gives each person free will. But He limits His exposure to people who are behaving poorly. There are times that God gets angry with people because of their disloyal and evil ways, and so He rejects them and removes them from His presence (Second Kings 17:17–19). God takes a stand against things that destroy love. Sometimes we have been conditioned on how we are to continue in our relationships with hurtful people.

Since God Himself has set the standard of removing one's presence, we are to follow His lead and limit our exposure to wicked people. Hopefully, the absence of relationship will cause them to question what they are missing and why they are missing it.

We also need to be able to set limits within ourselves. We need to allow ourselves the opportunity to have feelings without acting on them. That is the fruit of self-control. We need to be able to say "No" to ourselves. This includes both our destructive desires and some good ones that are not wise to pursue at a given time.

After months of not seeing and talking to Charles, I missed him and wanted to talk to him, but God said "No." He said "hands off." It was time for Him to work on Charles. I needed to be still. And as much as I wanted to hear his voice, I had to exert self-control and follow God's instructions to not call Charles or try to see him.

God's ways are such good examples of how we should live. The Bible is our blueprint, but we have to open it up and read the Word to know what it says so it can save us.

Isn't it beautiful that the Word tells us that God lets the repentant back into His presence (Mark 2:17, KJV). He doesn't let the person who simply says "I'm sorry" back. The difference between saying "I'm sorry" and being repentant is huge. You only speak words when you say you are sorry. Repentance is something you *do*. Repentance is saying "I'm sorry," but it goes a step farther. You see evidence of change in a person's sinful behavior. Second Chronicles 7:14 says, "If my people, who are called by my name, will humble themselves and pray and seek my face and turn from their wicked ways, then will I hear from heaven and will forgive their sin and will heal their land." A turning from wickedness occurs with being repentant.

First Corinthians 5:9–13 says,

> I have written you in my letter not to associate with sexually immoral people—not at all meaning the people of this world who are immoral, or the greedy and swindlers, or idolaters. In that case you would have to leave this world. But now I am writing you that you must not associate with

anyone who calls himself a brother but is sexually immoral or greedy, an idolater or a slanderer, a drunkard or a swindler. With such a man do not even eat.

What business is it of mine to judge those outside the church? Are you not to judge those inside? God will judge those outside. Expel the wicked man from among you.

There was a time when men would have sex with the women in the streets and then when they were ready to get married, they would go to the church to find a wife. Now churchwomen do every sexually immoral thing just like the women in the streets, and we wonder why we can't get married. It was never suppose to be this way. It's not the men who have changed. It's God's daughters who have lowered their standards, and He is trying to get our attention and tell us to come back to Him. We must turn from our wicked ways. Until then, we get what we get. God is judging us.

## TALENTS

Contrast these two responses:

Matthew 25:23 says, "Well done, good and faithful servant! You have been faithful with a few things; I will put you in charge of many things. Come and share your master's happiness!"

Matthew 25:26–28 says, "You wicked, lazy servant! So you knew that I harvest where I have not sown and gather where I have not scattered seed? Well then, you should have put my money on deposit with the bankers, so that when I returned, I would have received it back with interest. Take the talent from him and give it to the one who has the ten talents."

God has given all of us purpose and a mission. The mission is ours if we choose to accept it. When we are fruitful for the Kingdom of Heaven, God is pleased with us. He is the one we want to say to us, "Well done." Whether or not we get those kudos from others does not take precedent over God being pleased with what we do with what He has gifted us with. When we are good stewards with our talents, we are given more responsibility. God expands our territory, and we share in our master's happiness. But when we are lazy in God's eyes so that His Kingdom does not grow, the territory we had is taken away. Our talents are our responsibility, and we are to see them as such.

We are not only accountable but much happier when we are exercising our gifts and talents and being productive. We may face fear in our Kingdom-building efforts, but we are assured God will be with us. We are to confront our fears with help from God, who makes us over-comers and fruitful. God has given us the talent, and His grace will sustain us as we do the work.

I had never in a million years thought I would write a book, but God said to write down my experiences, and I did. He wanted me to have faith in Him that He would see me through. He would provide as only He could. Was there fear? Yes. Was there doubt? Yes. *But God!* I just did my part, and He put people in place who helped me make my thoughts into something tangible.

## THOUGHTS

Our minds and thoughts are important reflections of the image of God. No other creature on earth has our thinking ability. Created in God's likeness, the closer we get to Him, the more like Him we become. We are the only creatures who are called to love God with all our mind (Mark 12:30). Paul said in Second Corinthians 10:5 that he was taking captive every thought to make it obedient to Christ.

Establishing boundaries in thinking involves certain important things. *We must own our thoughts.* God tore the kingdom away from

# WHAT ARE BOUNDARIES

King Solomon because he allowed the women he married to turn his heart away from the true God and go after other gods, even though God had appeared to him and told him not to marry those women. King Solomon was responsible for his thoughts and suffered the consequences of being influenced by others to do wrong. *We must examine what others are telling us based on the truth we know.* Certainly, we should listen to the thoughts of others and weigh them, but we should never give our minds over to anyone.

God gave us a mind to think for ourselves. Peter was a guy I dated after Charles and before Kirk. I met Peter at a mixer, and he was nice enough. I wasn't physically attracted to him, but I was willing to get to know the young man. The first time he came over, we went to the mall and walked and talked. I tried on a dress and said I would go back and purchase it after it went on sale. Well, the next time Peter and I went out, it was to III Forks, a five-star steakhouse in Dallas. When he arrived at my apartment, he had a bag in his hand and told me to try on what was in the bag. It was the dress. I was really surprised and flattered. We had a lovely time together. I thought I could get used to this. It was like a fairy tale.

Peter would call and want to spend every day of the weekend together. He even wanted to do a weekend getaway together. Remember, I had just met him, and he had told me while talking about the last girl he dated, that they had just met and he had taken her away on a weekend trip where they had slept together. Now he wasn't interested in her any more. He told me how she always wanted to come over to his place and she didn't give him room to breathe. It was like she was suffocating him with her presence.

As he was telling me this, I was thinking, *It won't be me. I can learn from her mistake.* And I did. I would not be spending all of my time with him. I would not be going away on weekend trips with him since I didn't even know this man.

One evening, we had gone bowling and to dinner and we were talking at his place. I saw a gift box by his fireplace. The gift box was positioned so I could see it, and I felt he wanted me to ask him about the box. But I thought, *If he wants me to have what is in the box, he will give it to me. I don't have to ask for it.* He didn't mention anything about the box, and I didn't either.

He wanted to kiss me good night, and I told him to kiss me on the cheek. I wasn't feeling him like that. As I was leaving, Peter was insistent he kiss my lips. Now I had told him "No" already, but when he walked me to the car, he kissed me on the lips anyway.

I left and wrote him an e-mail, telling him he didn't respect my wishes and I couldn't see him anymore. It seemed to me he felt he had spent some money on me and now I owed it to him to do what he wanted me to do, but I didn't see a dollar sign anywhere on my body. I hope he didn't see one. If he did, oh, well ... rude awakening, because sister-girl cannot be bought. You have your thoughts, and I have mine. If you want to give to me, fine—give from your heart and not with expectation. Spending money on a woman was Peter's modus operandi. He spent money on you to get what he wanted.

I think we as women do this quite often. We give our bodies in expectation of a committed relationship, and when a man takes what we give, his intentions aren't to make us his girlfriend, companion, or wife. He took our precious body *because we gave it to him*.

Let me say it this way: Imagine you meet a guy. You date for a day or a week or a month, and he gives you the keys to his car. Now his car is a Mercedes Benz and is valuable to him, and he gives the car to you to drive for the week. You take the keys and enjoy the car. When you return the car, he is now claiming you are his girl and you both should date exclusively, but you aren't feeling him like that. By him giving you something he holds valuable, it doesn't mean you want to settle down with him and one day make him your husband and the father of your children. You took the car because he gave it to you.

Well, men will take "the precious" because we give it to them, but it doesn't mean they consider us their girlfriend or that they want to date us exclusively or that one day they will want to marry us. Don't devalue yourself by giving your pearls to swine. He cannot have "the precious" unless he is married to you.

Then there are times when we think we owe men because they took us to a nice restaurant or did something special for us. Don't put a price tag on yourself. God's Word says to owe no man anything but to love him (Romans 13:8, KJV). You don't owe that man anything but godly love. Don't think you have to pay him back. He should do what is in his heart to do. What he gives you should not be conditional, based on what you are going to do for him in return. And if he seems to think you owe him something, simply take him to task and ask him about it. "So you bought me dinner, and now you feel I *owe* you? I thought you were giving to me because you wanted to, not in expectation of something in return. What's up with that?"

We must grow in knowledge and expand our minds. One area in which we need to grow is in knowledge of God and His Word. King David said in Psalm 119:20, 24, "My soul is consumed with longing for your laws at all times ... Your statutes are my delight; they are my counselors." Whether we are doing brain surgery, balancing our checkbook, or raising children, we are to use our brains to have better lives and glorify God. We are to be like Christ and grow in wisdom. Luke 2:52 says, "And Jesus grew in wisdom and stature, and in favor with God and men." Are *you* growing in wisdom?

It behooves us to read self-help books and take classes that encourage our growth. If you are about to purchase a home, read a book on house buying to better prepare yourself. If you are having trouble staying organized or having trouble with overspending, you may consider taking a class on the matter. We should seek to improve and to learn something every day. Knowledge only makes our lives better. The Bible says we perish for lack of knowledge (Hosea 4:6).

We must clarify distorted thinking. If we are facing problems in our lives, these problems are trying to tell us something. It is our responsibility to seek a solution. What we feed our minds with can make us strong or weak. Jesus taught the disciples first, then he told them to go out and teach others (Matthew 28:18–20). *They were taught first.* The knowledge should transform us, THEN we are able to teach others. Taking ownership of our thinking in relationships requires being active in checking out where we may be wrong. As we gather new information, our thinking adapts and grows closer to reality. We must be intentional and deliberate in gaining wisdom. The question is: are *you* teachable?

It is also imperative that we communicate our thoughts to others. Often we think others should know what is on our mind, but the Word is clear that it is *our* responsibility to communicate our thoughts. Frustration can build when we don't communicate. Paul taught in First Corinthians 2:11, "For who among men knows the thoughts of a man except the man's spirit within him?"

While we were dating, Charles would reluctantly go places with me. I was the planner, and I primarily suggested places to go and things to do. Now that I think about it, Charles was content going to the gym to work out, watching TV, playing basketball, having sex, and doing the same thing day after day. He wasn't a person who liked to go to different places. He was content at home. I thought if I showed him how much fun it was to do different things, he would be as willing to go as I was. But that's not who he was, and I needed to accept him for who he was and not who I wanted him to be. This was a huge lesson. And in accepting him for who he was and what he liked would keep me from expecting him to do things he just didn't want to do, and then nagging him when he didn't do what I wanted him to do. He had shown me who he was and what he liked. I needed to see it and accept it.

Communication is key in relationships. I would have a problem with Charles and instead of talking to him about the problem, I would share my concerns with my girlfriend. He had no idea how I felt about some issues. I had tried to talk to my ex-husband, and it didn't seem to work, so I thought, *What's the use?* But Antonio and Charles were two totally different people. Charles would tell me a closed mouth doesn't get fed. He was encouraging me to tell him what was on my mind. He couldn't know any other way.

I can imagine that Charles was pretty disillusioned with me when I would walk away from the relationship without explaining what my displeasure was. How was he to know if I didn't tell him? I never told him how I felt about him looking at other women. I never told him about his flirting. I never told him about his lack of follow-through. I didn't ask him why he would mention going somewhere and not finalize the plans. How was he to know these things upset me—if I didn't tell him? By not saying anything, in essence, I was telling him I was okay with his behavior.

I know some of you will think that a man knows he shouldn't flirt with other women in front of you. That's common sense, right? But what if he thinks he's being friendly? Until you talk about it and get some understanding, you will not know why a person does what he does. The Bible continues to tell us to communicate with one another.

First Corinthians 14:20 (KJV) says, "Brethren, be not children in understanding: howbeit in malice be ye children, but in understanding be men." The Bible is telling us to act like children when we feel malice between each other. Children forgive and forget easily. We are to be adults and mature and seek to get an understanding of the issues we are facing.

## DESIRES

Our desires lie within our boundaries. Each of us has different desires and wants, dreams and wishes, goals and plans, hungers and thirst. We all have desires we would like to see come to fruition, but we often fail to take responsibility for our desires. A person desires companionship but perhaps doesn't act on an invitation they have been given or they fail to connect with a person they recently met. They may say they want to get out of the house and socialize, but there is no effort to obtain their desire. Too often, we have a desire, but we don't work to accomplish it. We remain unsatisfied because of our lack of initiative. Proverbs 13:19 (KJV) tells us, "A desire accomplished is sweet to the soul."

We hold ourselves back when we don't give attention and effort to what we want. We can stand in our own way and prevent ourselves from living productive, fulfilled lives. Is there initiative behind your desire?

God loves to give gifts to His children, but He is a wise parent. He wants to make sure His gifts are right for us. To know what to ask for, we have to be in touch with who we really are and what our real motives are. If we are merely wanting something to feed our pride or to enhance our ego, I doubt God is interested in giving it to us. But if it would be good for us, He's very interested.

For a long time, I had a desire to be married, but God knew I needed to mature in my walk with Him before He would satisfy that desire. My motives for wanting to get married were to have someone to love and do things with. The only problem was when I had someone in my life, I put them before the Father. God wanted me to correct this behavior before I received my blessing.

If you desire to be married, what is your motivation for wanting it? Are you only thinking about what someone can do for you, as I was, or are you thinking of how your marriage could glorify God and build His kingdom? We need to take a look at our motives, which are sometimes initiated out of fear. Our motives may be driven by fear of being alone. When we confess our motives and ask God to give us a pure heart, He will surely do it.

## LOVE

One of the greatest gifts God has given us is our ability to give and respond to love. The heart that God has fashioned in His image is the center of our being. Its abilities to open up to love and to allow love to flow outward are crucial to life. Matthew 22:37, 39 says, "Love the Lord your God with all your heart and with all your soul and with all your mind ... Love your neighbor as yourself."

Second Corinthians 6:11–13 reveals how we should receive love. "We have spoken freely to you, Corinthians, and opened wide our hearts to you. We are not withholding our affection from you, but you are withholding yours from us. As a fair exchange—I speak as to my children—open wide your hearts also."

We learn from Paul's statement to the Corinthians that love is to be given and received. Often from past fears and hurts, people shut themselves off from giving and receiving love. Our loving heart needs to be healed from past hurts so that we can give and receive love in order to grow and have healthy, happy relationships. Working our heart muscle allows it to grow strong and healthy, bringing love and joy into our lives. Unused, our love grows dull and lifeless.

We need to take responsibility for this loving function of ourselves and use it. Both, love concealed or love rejected can kill us.

Many people do not see how they reject love. God had been loving to the Israelites, but they continued to complain in spite of His goodness, acting like victims until they finally rejected God (First Samuel 8:7). Their rejection of God's goodness only hurt them. They were the ones who went without. They did not enter His rest.

One way to see the goodness of another is to acknowledge what they have done. Jesus teaches us to be thankful for the goodness of others and not take their goodness for granted. Luke 17:11–19 teaches,

> Now on his way to Jerusalem, Jesus traveled along the border between Samaria and Galilee. As he was going into a village, ten men who had leprosy met him. They stood at a distance and called out in a loud voice, "Jesus, Master, have pity on us!"
>
> When he saw them, he said, "Go, show yourselves to the priests." And as they went, they were cleansed.
>
> One of them, when he saw he was healed, came back, praising God in a loud voice. He threw himself at Jesus' feet and thanked him—and he was Samaritan.
>
> Jesus asked, "Were not all ten men cleansed? Where are the other nine? Was no one found to return and give praise to God except this foreigner?" Then he said to him, "Rise and go; your faith has made you well."

How are you rejecting love? Do you see the goodness of others and respond to their love? Or have you lost loving relationships because of your unresponsiveness? Are you lonely because you choose to be?

## WHAT ARE BOUNDARIES

God showed me how He blesses women with children. Often, these women are looking for love. They are specifically looking for a man's love. God wants them to know He loves them and has put unconditional love into their lives they overlook every day which is their beautiful children. Start loving the people with whom God has blessed you. Open your eyes and see all of the love that surrounds you every day. Love from where you are, and He will surely expand the love in your life.

Become aware of the love that is in your life and respond to that love. You, and only you, are responsible for what is inside your boundaries. If someone else is controlling your love, emotions, or values, they are not the problem. *Your* inability to set limits on their control is the problem. Boundaries are the key to keeping your very soul safe, protected, and growing.

# 8

## My Lack Of Boundaries

Since I have come to understand what boundaries are and the role they play in my life, I am thankful and grateful for my dating experience because now I have found wisdom which is more precious than choice gold.

On Wednesday nights, I would want to go hear the spoken Word or take swing-out dance lessons, or go to a health expo, but Charles wouldn't want to go for whatever reason and I would get pissed. I didn't understand why he wouldn't want to go to these fun places with me. It seemed that mostly what he wanted to do was have sex—and don't get me wrong, at that time, it was the best sex I had ever had so I wasn't complaining about the sex, it was the lack of activity outside of the bedroom that I missed.

I didn't feel used when we had sex because he was doing things and pleasing me in ways I had never experienced. He knew of my lack of experience, and now, I believe that putting it down on me like that was his modus operandi to get me hooked. It worked. He used his sexual talents to get me so in love with the sex that I was hooked.

Never having been a sexual person, I wanted more and needed

more from a relationship. I would ask him, "What else you got?" There had to be more—more than sex, I mean. Well, what I learned about my boundary problem was that it was my desire, my want to have him go with me, and only I am responsible for my wants. I can't control what he does with his time. If he chooses to go with me, then that is his choice; if not, that's OK as well. I can't make a person do something he doesn't want to do. I must respect his wants, or else I am trying to control him.

I see now that I had a problem with saying "No" and hearing "No." I don't want someone controlling what I do. I have to see things from that person's perspective, not just my own.

Everyone has the freedom of choices. I have choices. When you force someone to do something, you eventually push them away. I could have chosen to go with someone else. I could have chosen to go by myself. I could have mentioned how much it meant to me that he go with me and still given him the freedom to tell me "No." To nag him was just to make him resent me for the pressure I was putting on him.

God does not nag or beg us to do anything. He wants us to go and assemble together, but He doesn't nag us or make us go. God gives us choices. Since I am made in His likeness and I am His child, it is out of order to not respect someone else's freedom and choices. I would certainly want that other person to respect my freedom and choices when I don't want to go somewhere or do something.

I didn't want Charles dating anyone else. I felt since we were having sex and had been dating for a while we should be exclusive. That's how dating was suppose to be, right? That's what my small-town Phenix City, Alabama, mentality thought. I couldn't conceive of dating more than one person. You dated one person in order to see if you liked them enough to love them and marry them. Why have all of the other distractions? Well, those were my thoughts and feelings, and they weren't shared by Charles. That angered me, and I would break up with him over that issue. But I would soon go back because I didn't want to be by myself.

I later learned that dating multiple people was a choice he had made for himself. I needed to realize and understand that was his choice and accept the fact that he wanted to date multiple women. After being told his dating preferences, it was up to me to exercise my choices. I could have continued to date him with sex. I could have dated him without sex, or I could have dated him as well as others. Or I could have ceased to date him altogether. We both had freedom to choose what was right and best for our lives. I had no right trying to control his dating habits. I had a right to express my feeling about the matter. But that's all. I couldn't change who he was. I can only change me.

After experiencing the mind-blowing sex, the bike rides, fishing trips, meeting his family, going on vacations, working out at the gym, days of good and bad, I was ready for things to be over between Charles and me. I had had enough of his disappearing acts and his lack of commitment. All I wanted was for him to say it was over between us.

What I wanted was for him to tell me the truth about how he actually felt about me. I deserved to know the truth so I could move on with my life. I wanted him to say the relationship was over because when I said I was finished with him, I would end up going back. I wasn't strong enough to make the breakup last.

One evening we went out for dinner just to talk about where the relationship was headed. I was paying close attention because I needed to know. When he dropped me off at home, I asked him, "So do you want to stay in this relationship or not?" His reply was, "I told you, you just weren't listening." I thought about that all night. I didn't remember him saying anything about our future together or apart. He hadn't said anything.

It wasn't until much later as I was recalling that night that I understood it wasn't his words I was to listen to. It was his actions.

His noncommitment was speaking volumes. His behavior had told me all I needed to know, but I didn't understand at the time. I was listening, but I didn't like what I was hearing. I didn't want to believe what reality was telling me. I was only fooling myself. I was in denial. I was feeling distant from him, hence, the dinner to discuss the relationship.

Charles went MIA. He was missing in action. He didn't call as frequently as he used to. He didn't come by as often either. I realize now that sometimes it's hard for a person to break your heart with the words. In hindsight, I would have preferred he told me the truth. I felt he owed me that much, but I owed myself more. I owed it to myself to be real with myself and see things for what they were. The relationship was over.

I am sure when I displayed this unconcerned behavior with Kirk, he wished I would have just told him how I actually felt instead of stringing him alone. He was my rebound and interim. Eventually, I did tell Kirk I still had feelings for Charles and we could no longer see each other. I remembered how it felt to be strung along and realized I hadn't liked that feeling, so why would I think Kirk would. He deserved to know the truth. I had to be honest enough to tell him. If I mistreated him, I can expect someone to mistreat me in the future.

From this experience, I also learned to watch my boyfriend's actions. They tell me much more than words could ever say. Even God's Word tells us to be aware of a person's fruit. What kind of fruit does the guy I'm dating produce in our relationship? Is he helping me become a better person, or is he disrespectful, hurtful, and competitive? After I have told him about his behavior, does he remain unchanged? Then, I have to accept him for who he is and not for who I want him to be.

# 9

# The Change In Me

I needed to understand some very important things so my next relationship could be all that it was designed to be. I had already taken a look at my past to see my mistakes. Now I needed to make choices about where I was going with my future relationships. Was I going to put what I had learned into action?

## PUT GOD FIRST

In putting God first, I would spend quality time with Him. My favorite activity was walking in the morning. There was something special about watching a beautiful sunrise and thanking God for all He had done. I would read His Word. I found the stories in the Bible fascinating. The more I read, the more I understood who God was and how to be a better person. The Bible was my road map. I would discover so much about relationships when I read the stories of Jacob and Rachel and saw how Jacob worked for seven years for Rachel's father so he could marry her. Then there was the story of Boaz and Ruth and how Boaz provided for her and she allowed him to do that. Another wonderful story was about Moses and Zipporah. It told of how Moses' wife saved his life because of her obedience in spite of his disobedience.

All of these beautiful stories showed me the difference in the world's view on relationships and God's way. Another beautiful story concerns Queen Esther and her husband, the king. She was in the right place at the right time, and God used her to save a nation. There is also the story of Nabal and Abigail and how Abigail made peace with King David after her husband had disrespected him. In doing so, she saved all the males in the kingdom.

God wants us to have loving relationships. He gives us example after example of how to do so, but it is up to us to take the time and learn His ways or we can continue to do what we do and get what we get. The choice is yours. Choose who you will serve. I would have you choose the way of the Lord this day, but as for me and my house, we will serve the Lord (Joshua 24:15).

The man you are dating is no big deal. We make a mistake when we put men on a pedestal. God is the Big Deal. Men are children of God, and we are to treat them as such, not as gods. The man is not our savior, whether he is a professional athlete, singer, doctor, or preacher. It doesn't matter to us because we know whatever he has is a blessing from God and we need to look at the fruit of the spirit of the man instead of his possessions. Is he kind? How does he treat his mother and his children? Is he thoughtful or selfish? Galatians 5:22 tells us the fruit of the Spirit is love, joy, peace, patience, kindness, goodness, faithfulness, gentleness, and self-control. Against such things there is no law.

Understand when you do things God's way there will be guys who flee the scene. That is a good thing. The biblical process removes weeds in our life. Matthew 13:41–43 says,

> The Son of Man will send out his angels, and they will
> weed out of his kingdom everything that causes sin and all

who do evil. They will throw them into the fiery furnace, where there will be weeping and gnashing of teeth. Then the righteous will shine like the sun in the kingdom of their Father. He who has ears, let him hear.

As you grow spirituality, you will want to surround yourself with likeminded people who are also growing in biblical wisdom. Your Bible-based knowledge will give you confidence because you now know the truth and can live by biblical standards regardless of what others think and do. You can now live by God's rules and not some man's. There is instant respect when a woman can hold her own because her foundation is sure. And the man God has for you will love this about you. He will love that you aren't easily swayed in your thinking. He will adore that you have an opinion of your own. He will admire that he can't change your mind on things God has said for you to do or not to do. He will be wowed by your God-given strength, confidence, and freedom. You will be living God's standards and not anyone else's. This is true beauty.

Because you are now putting God first, you no longer seek to impress a man. You desire to impress your Father, who is the giver of every good and perfect gift. When we understand this truth, it frees us from being in competition with other women. What God has for me is for me. Not you. And what God has for you is for you. Not me. You are no longer desperate. If your man wants to date other women, he can go ahead because you are trusting God for your mate. If he wants to leave the relationship, he can go because you are trusting God for your happiness, peace, and joy. And when he misbehaves, you can confront him about his bad behavior with truth and mercy because now you are knowledgeable about the correct way he should be handling himself.

There is no more fear in your relationships. You do not fear being without him. You've got God. You do not fear some woman taking him. You've got God. You do not fear where he is or who he is with because God has given you a peace that surpasses all understanding. You won't feel a need to overcompensate or feel too eager to please because you know the woman's role and the man's role. But when we don't know these things and walk in them, we get role reversal, where the woman is providing all the income and the man is playing the PlayStation all day. God has a plan, and His way transcends all generations.

## I DEDICATED MY BODY TO GOD AND LIVED IN ABSTINENCE

I realize being abstinent is a good thing for us. To abstain from sex is a sacrifice. I gave my body back to God to do with as He saw fit. I am a workman for His glory not my own. I became a living sacrifice in that I wanted to have sex, I thought about it, but I said "No"—"No" to myself. I wanted the blessings for my life not the curses. It made sense to abstain from sex once I understood the reason God had me to abstain.

Delaying sex until marriage allows me to get to know the person I am dating. It shows me if we can relate to each other outside of the bed. How do we communicate? How do we problem solve? What are his values on saving money? What are his child-rearing techniques? Is he a workaholic? Does he disrespect me when other women are around? It is much easier to leave a relationship if there is evidence of blatant disrespect when there has been no sexual contact.

The Word tells us not to feed the dogs or give our pearls to swine. How many times have you or a friend had sex with a man and wished you hadn't? How many times have you had sex with a man, hoping he would one day marry you, and he didn't? Sex isn't a prerequisite for marriage as the world would have you believe. Just take a look around. Men will brag about how this woman did this for him and that woman performed this on him, but have you noticed after all she did for him and to him that he *still* didn't marry her?

It also helps to understand men. When a man wants a lady, he'll go after her, and going after her makes him want her even more. If he doesn't succeed in getting her attention right away, he starts to crave her. She captures his curiosity and stimulates his imagination. This being said, don't be so easy.

## FORNICATION

Fornication is having sex when you are not married. First Corinthians 6:13–20 (KJV) says,

> Meats for the belly, and the belly for meats: but God shall destroy both it and them. Now the body is not for fornication, but for the Lord; and the Lord for the body.
>
> And God hath both raised up the Lord, and will also raise up us by his own power.
>
> Know ye not that your bodies are the members of Christ? Shall I then take the members of Christ, and make them the members of an harlot? God forbid.
>
> What? Know ye not that he which is joined to an harlot is one body? For two, saith he, shall be one flesh.
>
> But he that is joined unto the Lord is one spirit.
>
> Flee fornication. Every sin that a man doeth is without the body; but he that committeth fornication sinneth against his own body.
>
> What? Know ye not that your body is the temple of the Holy Ghost which is in you, which ye have of God, and ye

are not you own?

For ye are bought with a price: therefore glorify God in your body, and in your spirit, which are God's.

I had been blocking my own blessing with my disobedience. Charles was a gift, and because of my behavior, our relationship was under a curse. Instead of giving him sex, I should have been sharing with him the Word of God. We should have been growing spiritually not sexually. God tells me to edify my brother. He tells me to love my neighbor as myself. And that love shows up when I love myself enough to seek God's Word and will for my life and to do the same for my neighbor. Now that is true love. If, in the end, Charles was not the one meant for me, then, oh, well, he would have been made a better person because of the experience, and I would have been as well.

We reap what we sow. If I sow a seed in him, and he marries someone else and blesses them, that is wonderful. God's will be done. Not mine. God will provide my blessing. Too often we do not do things God's way. Wouldn't you rather have a man who is about God's business instead of only sexing you up? Well, then, do your part and take him to the feet of Jesus. Matthew 4:4 (KJV) says, "But he answered and said, 'It is written, Man shall not live by bread alone, but by every word that proceedeth out of the mouth of God.'"

So often we want to make the relationship about us and what we can get out of it. God would have us make our relationships about Him. "God, you put this person in my life for a reason. What would you have me say to him or do for him?" God wants us to manage our relationships in a way that honors Him.

When Jesus talked about managing something, he was usually referring to a servant who had been entrusted by his master with certain resources and responsibilities (e.g., Luke 12:42). The Bible calls such a person a steward, or one who is not suppose to manage things for his own pleasure, convenience, or benefit. Instead, he is expected to follow his master's instructions and look out for his master's interests, even if they conflict with his own personal desires or convenience (John 12:24–26).

Understanding God's Word is an essential ingredient of wisdom, which is the ability to apply God's truth to life's complexities. Having wisdom does not mean you understand all of God's ways. It means you respond to life God's way (Deuteronomy 29:29). The better you know the Bible, the wiser you will be and the more effectively you will live a life of holiness.

Luke 12:42–48 says,

> The Lord answered, "Who then is the faithful and wise manager, whom the master puts in charge of his servants to give them their food allowance at the proper time? It will be good for that servant whom the master finds doing so when he returns. I tell you the truth, he will put him in charge of all his possessions. But suppose the servant says to himself, 'My master is taking a long time in coming,' and he then begins to beat the menservants and maidservants and to eat and drink and get drunk. The master of that servant will come on a day when he does not expect him and at an hour he is not aware of. He will cut him to pieces and assign him a place with the unbelievers.

> That servant who knows his master's will and does not get ready or does not do what his master wants will be beaten with many blows. But the one who does not know and does things deserving punishment will be beaten with few blows. From everyone who has been given much, much will be demanded; and from the one who has been entrusted with

much, much more will be asked.

One of the best ways to keep your focus on the Lord is to continually ask yourself, "How can I please and honor God in this situation?" In particular, "How can I bring praise to God by showing He has saved me and is changing me?" Seeking to please and honor God is a powerful compass for life, especially when we are faced with difficult challenges. Jesus himself was guided by these goals. In John 5:30, He said, "I seek not to please myself but him who sent me," and in John 8:29, He said, "The one who sent me is with me; he has not left me alone, for I always do what pleases him." Are you doing what pleases God or are you pleasing yourself?

## BEING CONTENT

This is a passage of scripture God gave me so I could learn to be content in my singleness and not be anxious while waiting for marriage. Philippians 4:4–13 (brackets added):

> Rejoice in the Lord always. I will say it again: Rejoice! Let your gentleness be evident to all. The Lord is near. Do not be anxious about anything, but in everything, by prayer and petition, with thanksgiving, present your requests to God. And the peace of God, which transcends all understanding, will guard your hearts and your minds in Christ Jesus.

> Finally, brothers, whatever is true, whatever is noble, whatever is right, whatever is pure, whatever is lovely, whatever is admirable—if anything is excellent or praiseworthy—think about such things. Whatever you have learned or received or heard from me, or seen in me—put it into practice. And the God of peace will be with you.

> I rejoice greatly in the Lord that at last you have renewed your concern for me. Indeed, you have been concerned,

but you had no opportunity to show it. I am not saying this because I am in need, for I have learned to be content whatever the circumstances. I know what it is to be in need, and I know what it is to have plenty. I have learned the secret of being content in any and every situation, whether well fed or hungry, whether living in plenty or in want [whether married or single]. I can do everything through him who gives me strength. (brackets added)

*Contentment* is independent of my circumstances. Our contentment is independent of what our date does or does not do. We find contentment whether we have a date or not. We are content whether someone asks us to dance or no one asks. Contentment is getting his call or not getting his call. God is in control of it all and gives me strength to live a fulfilled single life.

To find contentment, the first thing we can do is rejoice. Why can we rejoice? We can rejoice because God is good and blesses us all day, every day. It's up to us to see His blessings. We would feel so much better if instead of concentrating on what we do not have, we rejoiced in what God blesses us with.

How do we keep from being anxious? We pray about what we are feeling and going through. We put our petition before the Sovereign Lord. And don't forget to be thankful. By being thankful for what God does for us, we begin to see that we have so much to be thankful for. Then our few complaints take a backseat to our praises. What do we get when we do these things? The Word of God tells us we get a peace that surpasses all understanding. Isn't that where you want to be?

Another thing I would like to suggest is to ask God why you are not married. King David taught us when we have a question about why something is happening or not happening, we are to take our concern to the Father. "During the reign of David, there was a famine for three successive years; so David sought the face of the Lord" (Second Samuel 21:1). We simply say, "I want a husband. Why, Lord, don't I have a husband?" If you want to know why something is the way it is, seek God's face.

God's Word leads and guides us on how to live a life of contentment. Hebrews 13:1–6 says,

> Keep on loving each other as brothers. Do not forget to entertain strangers, for by so doing some people have entertained angels without knowing it. Remember those in prison as if you were their fellow prisoners, and those who are mistreated as if you yourselves were suffering.

> Marriage should be honored by all, and the marriage bed kept pure, for God will judge the adulterer and all the sexually immoral. Keep your lives free from the love of money and be content with what you have, because God has said, "Never will I leave you; Never will I forsake you." So we say with confidence, "The Lord is my helper; I will not be afraid. What can man do to me?"

We are to look at the men in our lives as our brothers instead of possible mates. When we see men as brothers, our entire outlook can change. We are then able to focus on what we can do for these men that would glorify God instead of wondering what they can do for us, like making us their wives. We would be able to speak a word into his life that would bless our brother instead of shying away because we like him and fear sharing that word with him.

Brotherly love is a wonderful and necessary thing to experience. How do women benefit from brotherly love? We allow ourselves male friends who look out for our best interests. Our male friends are able to give us brotherly advice with problems we are having in our relationships. Brotherly love allows us to have a male figure in our life we can relate to until our Boaz comes. These relationships keep us from becoming depleted of a male companion to the point that we are starving for male companionship and then overwhelm the next man who comes along.

Our male friends' love for us allows us to see how we can hope to be treated. They are our example. If the guy we are dating wants to leave us and the relationship, we are strong enough to let him go because he isn't the only source of male attention we have. Having male friends can keep your social calendar full.

To be content, it helps if you take the focus off yourself and help someone in need. You could join a prison ministry or volunteer with a local organization. When you help someone who is suffering, it allows you to have a better perspective on how blessed you truly are. What clothes, shoes, purses are you not using and haven't used in quite a while that you could give away to bless someone else? It would bless you to give away some of what you have. God blesses us so we will be a blessing to others. Where would He have you volunteer?

Are you content with what you have? Are you content with God? Why, or why not? Are you telling God He has not done enough for you with your attitude and lack of appreciation for what you have?

God wanted me to encourage you, as He has encouraged me. Isaiah 40:28–31 says,

> Do you not know? Have you not heard? The Lord is the everlasting God, the Creator of the ends of the earth. He will not grow tired or weary, and his understanding no one can fathom.
>
> He gives strength to the weary and increases the power of the weak.
>
> Even youths grow tired and weary, and young men

stumble and fall;

but those who hope in the Lord will renew their strength. They will soar on   wings like eagles; they will run and not grow weary, they will walk and not be faint.

Wait on the Lord's perfect timing to grant you a husband. So what can you do in the meantime? Some of the things I did in my meantime were: I took self-help classes at various churches, a sewing class, a cooking class, I vacationed, I volunteered, I went to jazz venues, museums, and singles' events. I worked on myself in the meantime: I went to plays, I went to wine tastings, I enjoyed life. I lived. I wrote this book.

One thing that helped me live a life of contentment was realizing that everything happens for God's glory. When I decided to accept this fact—that God has a plan—then I am able to accept things as they are. I would have to work at getting my mind around the fact that God loves me and has my best interests at heart even in my singleness, but with time, it got easier. I truly realize that God knows best and has a plan for my life.

If we think about it, there are a million things we want and long for, but if we focus on the positive, we easily realize we have a trillion things to be thankful for. It's all in how you look at your situation. It's your choice to be thankful and content.

I found myself being thankful for the small things, like getting to a play on time when I knew I had left my house late. I was thankful for getting a good parking space on a rainy day and not being in the traffic jam I saw heading in the opposite direction of the way I was going. I was thankful when He woke me up on time when I had forgotten to set my alarm. I was thankful for the time I found an umbrella in a shopping cart. The more I thanked Him, the more I became aware of all my many blessings.

# THE CHANGE IN ME

## HAVE PATIENCE

God wants us to have patience. He wants us to wait on Him, to wait on His perfect timing. As you grow in patience, you grow perfect and entire, wanting nothing. This is a wonderful place to be. James 1:2–4 (KJV) says, "My brethren, count it all joy when ye fall into divers [many] temptations; knowing this, that the trying of your faith worketh patience. But let patience have her perfect work, that ye may be perfect and entire, wanting nothing" (brackets added).

I can relate to wanting a husband "now." I remember after being married for one month shy of ten years, and after the relationship with Charles, I prayed, "Lord, send me my husband by the end of this week." I wanted him right then. What was the point in waiting? Growth!

My new saying is, "Jehovah-plus-one is enough." In case you are wondering, *I'm* the plus one. Knowing that I am never alone because my Father is always with me gives me an inward peace. Knowing that my Father is with me let's me know He cares about me and what I am going through. He is right there going through my situation with me.

## HAVING MY LIFE

You may have noticed that men keep their life routines. They still go and play basketball on the scheduled night or go to the football game or play pool. They rarely stop their routine activities for us. They usually make time for us when it's convenient for them. They fit us in. We can learn a lot from them.

I was at the gym one morning when I saw Charles' car as I was parking. I said a quick prayer as I was entering the gym. It's amazing what prayer can do. I don't remember the specific prayer, but it was for peace, strength, or for God to have mercy. Anyway,

# MY TESTIMONY

I saw Charles as I went to the women's change room. I kept my eyes forward and proceeded to where I was going. I finished my resistance training and went to the stair stepper. I kept my eyes on what I was doing the entire time so when he walked up to me, it was to my surprise. He smiled and spoke, and I spoke. He said he wanted to talk to me and I just looked at him. Finally, he asked me to call him. I looked harder and said, "You do it." He said okay, and I kept working out and didn't see him after that.

Will he call? I don't know. If he wants to talk to me, he should be the one to put forth the effort to get in touch with me. If I wanted to talk to him, then I would call him. But this is his desire and his responsibility. I am no longer taking responsibility for others' desires and wants if I can help it. I know I won't always get it right, but with God's help, I will get it right most of the time.

Men love to tell us to call them. We must understand we have a choice to call them or not. Patience is a virtue. It takes lots of patience and self-control to not pick up the phone and call. But one thing we must understand is that we participate in role reversal when we are pursuing the man by making most of the phone calls. At those times, we are the initiator instead of the man. This is detrimental to our relationships. We learn from the prophet Nathan how to encourage a man to handle his business. To show King David his responsibilities, Nathan tells him, "You are the man!" (Second Samuel 12:7). When a man wants me to do something he should be doing, I love to tell him to "you are the man" and handle his own business.

God taught me in His Word who I should put my trust in. Jeremiah 17:5–8 says,

> This is what the Lord says: "Cursed is the one who trusts in man, who depends on flesh for his strength and whose heart turns away from the Lord.

He will be like a bush in the wastelands; he will not see prosperity when it comes. He will dwell in the parched places of the desert, in a salt land where no one lives.

But blessed is the man who trusts in the Lord, whose confidence is in him.

He will be like a tree planted by the water that sends out its roots by the stream. It does not fear when heat comes; its leaves are always green. It has no worries in a year of drought and never fails to bear fruit."

We all know the desert is naturally hot. To be in a parched place in a desert is a really bad place to be. There is no relief. There is no end to your thirst. You may be looking for a relationship, but no one is around, or you may have a relationship, but it doesn't satisfy. Your predicament leaves you hot and bothered. If this is your situation, it may be because you have put your trust in a man and turned from the Lord.

But if your confidence is in the Lord, your thirst will be quenched. You will find relief. You will prosper. And if a man is not in your life for a season, it does not bother you because your trust is in the Lord. In your season of drought (having no man), you have no worries and you are still able to take care of business. Things around you are still growing, and your life is producing fruit.

So the next concern is, how much do we trust God? Do we really trust Him to supply all our needs? Do we trust His love for us and His knowledge of what the absolute best is for us, as well as for the one we love?

To the degree that we trust God and allow Him to direct our lives and our relationships, we can be free from the detriment of expectations and free to let the Lord love that person through us.

And if we can trust Him, we can then pray wholeheartedly for our friend's happiness, secure in the knowledge that God is going to fulfill all our needs (not necessarily all our wants), and we don't have to depend on a person to do it. We can say with our whole being, "I love you, and there are no expectations. I just want to be around to support you in whatever way the Lord wants me to. I want to pray for you, share your burdens, and be involved in your life because I love you, but I'm not expecting anything from you. I simply and truly want to see you happy and fulfilled." That is the pursuit of brotherly love. That is *serving* rather than *being served* and *loving* rather than *being loved*.

Prayer is such an unselfish act. Why don't you take a minute and pray for the men in your life right now? Are you able to pray for God's will to be done, and that He send the woman of His choice to the man you are dating? Why, or why can you not do this?

What if God had said that Charles was supposed to be someone else's husband? What if God had said I was to be someone else's wife? Was I to tell God "No"? This revelation gave me so much peace when a beautiful lady transferred to our work facility. She was pretty and had a nice shape—just the kind of woman Charles would be attracted to. I felt a pinch of jealousy when one of our coworkers introduced us, but as I drove down the street, a small voice said, "What if I have someone else for Charles to marry?" After thinking about it that way, I couldn't help but be fine with whatever God had planned because I know He is looking out for me as well. And His plans are the best-made plans. I love Him.

While driving to church one morning, I got a vision that I would be the one who would introduce Charles to the new young lady at work, and then I would walk away. I was okay with introducing them. I could see the introduction and was just fine. Because my hope is in Him, He gave me peace. He had once again worked it out. Sometimes we have to work things out in our heads, with God's help, of course. Let Him help you see the visions He has for your life. When there is no vision, walk in faith knowing He will make a way. Just believe His promises.

One day, I ran into the pretty, young controller at work. I felt a pinch of jealousy again. I really didn't want to feel this way. God asked me, "If you didn't feel the way you do for Charles, how would you treat her? If Charles wasn't a factor, how would you treat her?" I knew immediately. I would invite her to church and some of the single events that were happening around town. That was what I was to do—be my loving, caring self.

Another revelation God shared with me is that I have a double standard for my girlfriends and my guy friends. Girlfriends and guy friends do the same things. God showed me where my girlfriend Renea had sent an invitation asking if anyone wanted to go to the comedy house on Friday or Saturday. It was Wednesday when she sent out the invitations through e-mail. I replied I wanted to go and Saturday night worked better for me. Saturday came and went, and if I heard from Renea, you heard from Renea. I didn't call her because this was her idea and her plans. I was not jumping for the carrot she had placed in front of me. I was not going to take over and plan things unless she asked me to, and she hadn't. I knew she was capable of planning events. She worked at the church, and that's what she did all the time, make plans for youth events, senior events, and church conferences. She just didn't put the effort in planning this event.

I had a Plan B. I had seen this behavior in Renea in the past. There was no follow-through. She would mention something, and then I wouldn't hear from her, even after I had indicated I wanted to go. I didn't get bent out of shape or dismiss Renea because of it like I did my boyfriends when they didn't call. Why was that? Why do we have a double standard?

I know many women do the same thing. Is it because we have a purpose for these men that perhaps God doesn't have? Is it because we have expectations of a future with our male companion but we are not taking in consideration God's plans for them and us. If they were truly friends, it would be okay for them to call whenever they got around to it, as evidenced by our female friendships. Often the reason we get upset when they don't call is we are trying to make this guy our husband and not allowing him to be our friend. We want something to happen that maybe God doesn't want to happen. When we can say and mean it, "I want this man to be my husband, but nevertheless, God's will be done," we have arrived.

I had to realize Charles wasn't good at following through, and neither was Renea. If I wanted them to know how I felt, I should talk to them about their behavior and how it makes me feel. This behavior could be something that they are not aware of and that needs to be brought to their attention. I could say, "Why do you mention going bike riding but then don't make plans?"

It helps to know what you are dealing with. I realize they may call or they may not call, and I accept them for who they are, and I know to always have a backup plan.

The change happens with me when I have a Plan B. And I have to be aware of my attitude. There shouldn't be one standard for my female friends that says I'm okay with whenever she calls, but my male friends must call within a certain time frame.

One Friday night I spent time with one of my girlfriends, Val. She and I had gone to a singles' event at Concord Baptist Church in Dallas. As we were leaving, she asked if I wanted to see a movie on Saturday. I told her maybe. She said she would call me. I said okay. Needless to say, she did not call.

When I saw her that following Saturday night, we went to a jazz and spoken word event, and she asked what I had done earlier. I told her I had gone to a Delta luncheon and worked out. I asked her and she said she had gone to see the movie she had invited me to go to. I asked her how it was. It was no big deal that she had gone to see it without me. I didn't bagger her or nag her or end the relationship. Since she hadn't called me, I went ahead with what I had planned. My life is my responsibility. If only we could get to the point where we have this same disposition when men don't call— that it's no big deal—we would be better off. We don't have to get upset. I have learned how to not allow myself to become upset by people, places, things, or circumstances. They are powerless. My reaction is their only power.

God also let me see how I failed to call someone who I said I would call so we could get together. How can I be mad at anyone when I do the same thing myself? That plank in our eye compared to the splinter in the other person's eye is something else.

The beginnings of relationships are often the best times to be had by both people. I remember when Antonio and I first started dating. Everything was so calm and natural. We enjoyed bike riding, jazz, and talking. Things just flowed so effortlessly. Being together was easy.

When I was getting to know Charles, our relationship was effortless as well. We would talk about everything from his childhood to his past relationships to his family. We enjoyed being together. We were friends first. Somewhere in the relationship, we lost the easiness. We lost the friendship. *Big mistake.* Could we ever go back to the things we did at first?

Antonio's proposal had completely caught me off guard. I had no idea he was thinking marriage. I look back on that time and realize he was thinking marriage and my state of mind was just in the enjoyment of the relationship. He was able to think about marriage because I wasn't. I wasn't throwing hints. I wasn't pressing the issue. I was just enjoying his company. Then out of nowhere, he proposed.

Think back on your relationships and remember the person you were when he found you attractive. What was it about your personality that attracted you to him? Did he enjoy how easy it was to be in your company? Did he like that you were opinionated and told him to get in line when no one else had? Don't push him away with pressure. Don't make it hard for him to be around you. Remain friends. Relationships shouldn't be a struggle. You will have ups and downs. Those help you grow, but to be despised by a person because of the pressure you put on them to be with you is another situation entirely.

With Antonio, I cared about how he treated me when we were together. When he was not with me, I wasn't concerned about what he was doing. What he was doing when he wasn't with me was between him and God. Initially, that's how I felt about Charles. But as time went on, I let his antics get under my skin. I had to learn not to worry, because there was nothing, absolutely nothing, I could do about what he was doing anyway, so why worry? I had to trust that God would deal with whatever he was doing when he wasn't with me.

## LISTENING

I met Danny at Sweet Georgia Brown, a Black-owned and -operated restaurant in Dallas. I listened to Danny. I paid attention to what he was saying. He said people would get upset with him because they thought he would say hurtful things to them. He said he would later apologize. He wasn't afraid to say what was on his mind. In my mind, I was thinking, *Arquila, you have just been warned. The man is telling you what you need to know. You had better listen and pay attention so you won't say later, "I didn't know he was like that."* I had been forewarned of this guy's anger!

During one conversation, Danny asked what I was doing that evening. I told him I had plans and would be hanging out with friends. He then asked where I was going. I told him, "None of your business."

He said, "I'm going to let you make it this time."

I thought what he said was odd. I could hear a change in his voice, as if this could have been one of those times where he lashed out because he was angry at my response to him. I paid close attention to what he was saying and how it would affect me. I noticed his anger. I did not want to be with another man with whom I could not communicate.

There were pauses in our conversation, dead silence, and I was okay with the silence. After a while, Danny would bring up a topic. It's funny when you give a man a chance to talk by being quiet, he will find something to talk about. I felt he was asking me about my activities for the evening because he wanted to know if I was going to be depending on him for my social calendar. He wanted to know if I had a life, or if I would be one of those women calling him and hounding him so he would spend time with her. *Been there, done that.* Thank God for maturity.

Early on in the conversation, Danny asked if I had family here in Texas. I said "No." Then he wanted to know about my social circle. He was fishing. He was wondering if he was doing me a favor by being in my life because Black men are such a hot commodity—in their minds. He wanted to know if I would break down and ask him out or plan our first date. He just didn't know that I'm okay by myself—Jehovah plus one. I was fine before Danny came into my world, and I can live just fine now. He wanted to know if I was just sitting at home waiting on the opportunity to date. What a rude awakening: a single sister who is *not* going to chase you. I was so happy when God gave me this revelation. I can't take credit for what God did for me. That's discernment at its finest.

This is when self-control comes in. Even if I wanted him to take me out, I needed to practice self-control and not be so obvious with my feelings. It's like wanting to buy a car and when you see what you want, you jump up and down, saying, "I want it. I've got to have it." Well, the salesperson sees this behavior and thinks, *Got her*. He knows you want what he has, and he is in the driver's seat.

Your desire is evident when you don't keep your emotions in check, because that's when you've shown him your hand. You have shown him how desperate you are. The car dealer could withhold the special offers because he knows you will do almost anything to get your ride. You've *got* to have it, and he knows, and now he has an advantage over the situation. If you saw the car you had to have and didn't let your emotions show how much you wanted it, you could remain cool, calm, and collected to the point where you could walk away from the deal, then the car salesman would be doing everything he could to make the sale.

Do you see the difference in the two scenarios? You felt the same way in each case, but you didn't let your deep desire be known in the second scenario. You didn't give the salesman an advantage by showing your hand. Your emotional state and behavior didn't give you away. You didn't let your emotions control you. You controlled your emotions, which put you in the driver's seat. It's the fruit of the spirit of self-control. Many of the men we date are in the driver's seat because we show them how badly we want them.

I had to really work on taking control of my emotions and not letting them control me. I am so emotional. I wear my feelings on my sleeve. I would practice breathing deeply to calm down and pause before I spoke. It took practice, practice, and more practice.

After knowing me for just a couple of days, Danny would talk about how I was going to be his woman. The same day I met this guy, he was saying in five years we would be laughing because he had told me when we met that we would be together five years later. Then he would say he wanted to spend time with me. If he called and didn't get a chance to talk to me, he would call the next day and say he had tossed and turned all night because he hadn't been able to talk to me. I got so tired of his play on words that I told him to quit with the Mack-Daddy bull crap. That's all it was. He felt all women wanted to be wanted by some man—any man—and this talk would seal the deal. He thought he was making headway by telling me he had missed talking to me and that he couldn't sleep because he hadn't talked to me. He thought his words would be enough to get in my mind and have me thinking *this man really cares for me*. But mind you, he hadn't done anything to show it. Danny's modus operandi was his use of words. He used them to get what he wanted.

He was saying what he thought would get him brownie points. Men will say what they think you want to hear in order for you to do what they want you to do. I was not falling for it.

He talked this Mack-Daddy talk for a week, then said he was waiting on me to tell him when we could have dinner. He would be waiting until the end of days because planning a date was his job, especially in the initial stages of our relationship. Men know how to plan. Don't let the naiveté fool you.

Start off like you expect to continue. If I make plans now, I will be planning from now on. He is the man, so he needs to wear the pants and plan a date.

The Word of God helps us to not be fooled by what people are telling us. Colossians 2:8 says, "See to it that no one takes you captive through hollow and deceptive philosophy, which depends on human tradition and the basic principles of this world rather than on Christ."

Danny's words were hollow and deceptive, but they would not be taking this sister captive. He used words to get what he wanted. How often do women find themselves captive in a pseudo relationship where we think the relationship is going somewhere because of what the man we are getting to know has said? There is *no evidence* of the relationship going anywhere. He is all talk. Be careful of a man's hollow and deceptive philosophy. Words without works are dead.

# 10

# What Lesson Is GOD Trying To Teach You?

There were certain areas where God wanted to mature me. I share them with you in hopes that we can grow together. God let me know that I could be handed over to Satan in order to be taught a lesson. *Who knew?*

First Timothy 1:18–20 says, "Timothy, my son, I give you this instruction in keeping with the prophecies once made about you, so that by following them you may fight the good fight, holding on to faith and a good conscience. Some have rejected these and so have shipwrecked their faith. Among them are Hymenaeus and Alexander, whom I have handed over to Satan to be taught not to blaspheme." I felt I had been handed over to Satan to be taught not to fornicate. I learned my lesson!

Have you rejected faith and a good conscience, and God has handed you over to Satan to be taught a lesson? Maybe your lesson is that you eat too much and are overweight and suffering because of your eating habits or lack of exercise. Maybe you aren't a good steward over the money with which God has entrusted you and now you are in debt. Maybe you are fornicating and experiencing one failed relationship after another. What has your life shipwrecked?

Growing up in my father's house with the verbal abuse made me afraid of confrontation. I did not want to get in trouble because it reminded me of the harsh words my father would say to me. God used these verses to help me deal with others' anger directed at me. Hebrews 11:24–27 says:

> By faith Moses, when he had grown up, refused to be known as the son of Pharaoh's daughter. He chose to be mistreated along with the people of God rather than to enjoy the pleasures of sin for a short time. He regarded disgrace for the sake of Christ as of greater value than the treasures of Egypt, because he was looking ahead to his reward. By faith he left Egypt, not fearing the king's anger; he persevered because he saw him who is invisible.

Moses did not fear the king's anger. This is a lesson for us because we often fear our boyfriends' anger. If we see Him who is invisible through faith, we are able to do what He says in spite of our boyfriends' anger. They can get upset all they want; we have an assignment to do. And we are not going to miss our assignment because of their anger. That anger is their issue. We will persevere. We will not change our God-ordained thinking because it upsets them.

Our boyfriends may get mad when we say no to sex. They may get angry when we tell them not to call at an indecent hour. They may pitch a fit when you make time for Bible study or your friends. They will probably get angry when you stand up and do what God has instructed you to do. It's okay that they get frustrated.

Just remember, when you are doing right, some people will become frustrated with you.

First John 4:18 says, "There is no fear in love. But perfect love drives out fear, because fear has to do with punishment. The one who fears is not made perfect in love."

## DO YOU HAVE WHAT IT TAKES TO BE A GODLY WOMAN?

God has told us in His Word the characteristics that we should possess. I would like to share with you what He shared with me.

James 1:19–22 tells us,

> My dear brothers [and sisters], take note of this: Everyone should be quick to listen, slow to speak and slow to become angry, for man's anger does not bring about the righteous life that God desires. Therefore, get rid of all moral filth and the evil that is so prevalent and humbly accept the word planted in you, which can save you.

Do not merely listen to the word, and so deceive yourselves. Do what it says.

How many times will you find yourself in the same situation because you have not accepted God's Words for your life? You hear, but you do not obey, then you wonder what's wrong. God is trying to tell you to obey Him.

We will face certain situations with men. The Word is telling us to be prepared and be thoughtful. Don't be caught off guard every time something happens to you. If you see something once, learn what worked and what didn't work, because that scenario is bound to come around again. First Peter 1:13–16 says,

> Therefore, prepare your minds for action; be self-controlled; set your hope fully on the grace to be given you when Jesus Christ is revealed. As obedient children, do not conform to the evil desires you had when you lived in ignorance. But just as he who called you is holy, so be holy

in all you do; for it is written: "Be holy, because I am holy."

Verse 22 continues with this exhortation, "Now that you have purified yourselves by obeying the truth so that you have sincere love for your brothers, love one another deeply, from the heart."

God wants His daughters to be good judges of character with the people we meet. His Word lets us know what to pay attention to so we see the true character of a person. This keeps us from being fooled into believing something that is not true.

Matthew 12:35–37 (KJV) says,

> A good man out of the good treasure of the heart bringeth forth good things: and an evil man out of the evil treasure bringeth forth evil things.
>
> But I say unto you, That every idle word that men shall speak, they shall give account thereof in the day of judgment.
>
> For by thou words thou shalt be justified, and by thy words thou shalt be condemned.

This is how you know the spirit of a person. If the person is evil, you will see it if you pay attention. What is in a person's heart will spring forth. They can't conceal it forever. So when you say, "I didn't know he was this way," you didn't know because you *refused* to see the truth. The Bible tells us an evil man out of the evil treasure of his heart bringeth forth evil things. Pay attention. What do you see?

## ARE YOU SHOWING FAVORITISM?

If you are choosing a guy based on his status, his car, his clothes, his house, his job, his height, his skin color, his eyes, his build, then you are showing favoritism and judging. You may not have the blessed man God wants for you because you are excluding him.

# WHAT LESSON IS GOD TRYING TO TEACH YOU?

James 2:1–13 (brackets added) says,

> My brothers [and sisters], as believers in our glorious Lord Jesus Christ, don't show favoritism. Suppose a man comes into your meeting wearing a gold ring and fine clothes, and a poor man in shabby clothes also comes in. If you show special attention to the man wearing fine clothes and say, "Here's a good seat for you," but say to the poor man, "You stand there" or "Sit on the floor by my feet," have you not discriminated among yourselves and become judges with evil thoughts?
>
> Listen, my dear brothers [and sisters]: Has not God chosen those who are poor in the eyes of the world to be rich in faith and to inherit the kingdom he promised those who love him? But you have insulted the poor. Is it not the rich who are exploiting you? Are they not the ones who are dragging you into court? Are they not the ones who are slandering the noble name of him to whom you belong?
>
> If you really keep the royal law found in Scripture, "Love your neighbor as yourself," you are doing right. But if you show favoritism, you sin and are convicted by the law as lawbreakers. For whoever keeps the whole law and yet stumbles at just one point is guilty of breaking all of it. For he who said, "Do not commit adultery," also said, "Do not murder." If you do not commit adultery but do commit murder, you have become a lawbreaker.
>
> Speak and act as those who are going to be judged by the law that gives freedom, because judgment without mercy will be shown to anyone who has not been merciful. Mercy triumphs over judgment!

I have been there, and I can relate. Before I married my ex-husband, I would say I didn't want to marry a police officer or a man in debt—and he was both. And it wasn't those things that bothered me because our work schedules worked out just fine and I showed him how to pay off his debt and have good credit. That's what God does with our differences. Where I am weak, my man can show me a more excellent way. Where he is weak, I can teach him so we build each other up. You don't know what blessings you are passing over by being judgmental. God is still dealing with me in this area, because I still don't want a husband shorter than me or fat.

Now I see where those things shouldn't matter. If he loves me with the love of God, who cares how tall he is and I can coach him on becoming healthier.

Another situation where someone might show favoritism is with a specific race. Do not show favoritism. If God would have you marry someone of a different race or hue, would you tell God "No"? Sometimes we tell God "No" to His blessings because the man does not come in the package we thought he should. If God made every man who walks this earth and He doesn't see anything wrong with him, why do you? Why would you say he is the wrong shade when God created him that shade? Why would you say his eyes are too big when they are the eyes God gave him? Do you know better than God?

Well, what is a sister to do? I'm glad you asked. Ask God if this is the man for you. He will let you know. Just listen for His answer. Pay attention to the signs. God puts obstacles in our way to turn us in a different direction. Ezekiel 3:20 says, "Again, when a righteous man turns from his righteousness and does evil, and I put a stumbling block before him, he will die."

I remember calling Charles once. I was having a weak moment and just wanted to hear his voice. Do you know when I dialed his number I got a message saying his phone was not receiving calls. I had never heard that message ever. All I could say was, "Look at God." He knew I was having a weak moment. He also knew His plans for me. He didn't allow the call to go through. God blocked it. What is God blocking in *your* life? What is God telling *you* "No" to? He won't let you have what you want. He was saying, "No, Arquila, you are not to talk to him." The moment passed, and I felt better. We must see when and how God is graciously guiding our path.

## UNDERSTANDING GOD IS SOVEREIGN

It is for God to will and do as He pleases. We cannot without sinning say what we will do in the future (i.e., I will be married with children, I will be a doctor, I will purchase a house, I will go to college, I will go to church Sunday, I will wake up in the morning and cook breakfast). God is Sovereign and in control of the future, which is for Him to decide. We can only accept His will and His purpose. To say what you are going to do in the future is sinful. What can we control? What about the future can we say for certain is going to happen? Nothing. We are here today and gone tomorrow. That is why we should do what we can and leave the outcome to God. He knows what He is doing. We must trust that God knows. He has the big picture. This is huge because we can stop worrying about the outcome of situations and accept God's will—everything for His glory. So to pray for His will, to operate in His will, and leave the outcome of every situation to the Father of the universe is the thing to do.

I had to learn to say, "I *plan* to do this" or "I plan to do that." I can't say for certain anything about the future besides what God will allow.

James 4:13–17 says,

Now listen, you who say, "Today or tomorrow we will go to this or that city, spend a year there, carry on business, and make money." Why, you do not even know what will happen tomorrow. What is your life? You are a mist that appears for a little while and then vanishes. Instead, you ought to say, "If it is the Lord's will, we will live and do this or that." As it is, you boast and brag. All such boasting is evil. Anyone, then, who knows the good he ought to do and doesn't do it, sins.

Jesus taught His disciples, as He teaches us today, to pray for God's will to be done in our lives. Luke 11:1–4 (KJV) says,

And it came to pass, that, as he was praying in a certain place, when he ceased, one of his disciples said unto him, Lord, teach us to pray, as John also taught his disciples.

And he said unto them, When ye pray, say, Our Father which art in heaven, Hallowed be thy name. Thy kingdom come. Thy will be done, as in heaven, so in earth.

Give us day by day our daily bread.

And forgive us our sins; for we also forgive everyone that is indebted to us. And lead us not into temptation; but deliver us from evil.

Can you imagine that God's will might look different from your will? Well, it can. He teaches us that His ways are not our ways. His thoughts are not our thoughts. We must live in acceptance of God's will or live a life of frustration.

As I grew in understanding of God's will, I was able to pray as follows:

Lord, today I will live in acceptance. I will accept people, situations, circumstances, and events as they occur. I will accept that You have a purpose for my singleness. I will accept that You have a purpose for my pain. God, I will accept You are in control of it all. Everything happens to draw us closer to You. Everything happens so we might know You and feel Your love for us. And I'm okay with that. Lord, if the man I desire calls, I accept that. If he doesn't, I accept that. Not my will, but thine be done.

In faith lies the wisdom of uncertainty …

In the wisdom of uncertainty lies the freedom from our past, from the known, which is the prison of past conditioning. And in our willingness to step into the unknown, the field of all possibilities, we surrender ourselves to God's wisdom, which orchestrates the dance of the universe. We say, "I don't know what the future holds, but I trust God to work it out," which is the definition of faith. Hebrews 11:1 (KJV) says, "Now faith is the substance of things hoped for, the evidence of things not seen."

We are certain God will take care of us—him—and it—whatever it is. Faith is believing even though I may not see my husband, I see Him who is invisible. Faith says that in this circumstance I stay obedient because I believe God. Faith is not having what you want but believing God will provide for you. God will see you through. God has plans for me, plans to prosper me (Jeremiah 29:11), and I believe that.

God checks your attitude.

Numbers 14:20–25 *(The Life Recovery Bible)* says,

"Then the Lord said, 'I will pardon them as you have requested. But as surely as I live, and as surely as the earth is filled with the Lord's glory. Not one of these people will ever enter that land. They have all seen my glorious presence and the miraculous signs I performed both in Egypt and in the wilderness, but again and again they have tested me by refusing to listen to my voice. They will never even see the land I swore to give their ancestors. None of those who have treated me with contempt will ever see it. But my servant Caleb has a different attitude than the others have. He has remained loyal to me, so I will bring him into the land he explored. His descendants will possess their full share of that land. Now turn around, and don't go on toward the land where the Amalekites and Canaanites live. Tomorrow you must set out for the wilderness in the direction of the Red Sea."

In this passage, God has given Moses instructions concerning the Israelites who have complained ever since they were freed out of bondage. They had seen what God had done for them by sending the plagues upon Pharaoh and freeing them from slavery, but they still refused to listen to His instructions for their lives. Because they tested God and would not listen, that generation was denied access to the land flowing with milk and honey.

But Caleb had a different attitude. He had remained loyal to God and believed God would provide for them. Because of his attitude and loyalty, Caleb was going to receive the wonderful blessings God wanted to give him.

How is *your* attitude toward God and what He has done for you? Do you see all of the wonderful things He has done, and is doing, in your life? Are you thankful? Do you believe He has great things in store for you if you are loyal to Him? You may not have received your blessings because of your attitude.

# 11

## What Three Things Do You Need In A Man?

As a woman of God, you may have wondered at one time or another what a godly man looks like and what qualities he should possess. These passages were added so that we women will know what to look for in a man. We can also take these passages and share them with our brothers and sons so they, too, will know the right way to treat a lady. It's about maturity. The more we share these lessons with our brothers, sons, and friends, the more these characteristics are ingrained in them and in us. We aren't wondering about whether this is the man for us. God has told us how things should be in His Word, and He has told us what a godly man looks like.

The first area of concern deals with authority. Will he submit to authority? How does he get along with his boss at work? What kind of relationship does he have with his parents? Is he obedient to God?

You want a man who will submit to the authority God has placed over him. If he will not submit to authority, then *he* rules his house. If he submits to Christ, then *Christ* rules his house.

First Corinthians 11:3 (KJV) says, "But I would have you know, that the head of every man is Christ; and the head of the woman is the man; and the head of Christ is God."

The second area of concern is that the man needs to choose you. We all know that with the woman's movement and liberation, the world has changed, but God's way of doing business has not changed. His way is the same yesterday, today, and forever.

Genesis 29:1-35 tells us,

> Then Jacob continued on his journey and came to the land of the eastern peoples. There he saw a well in the field, with three flocks of sheep lying near it because the flocks were watered from that well. The stone over the mouth of the well was large. When all the flocks were gathered there, the shepherds would roll the stone away from the well's mouth and water the sheep. Then they would return the stone to its place over the mouth of the well. Jacob asked the shepherds, "My brothers, where are you from?"
>
> "We're from, Haran," they replied.
>
> He said to them, "Do you know Laban, Nahor's grandson?"
>
> "Yes, we know him," they answered.
>
> Then Jacob asked them, "Is he well?"
>
> "Yes, he is," they said, "and here comes his daughter Rachel with the sheep."
>
> "Look," he said, "the sun is still high; it is not time for the flocks to be gathered. Water the sheep and take them back to pasture."
>
> "We can't," they replied, "until all the flocks are gathered and the stone has been rolled away from the mouth of the well. Then we will water the sheep."
>
> While he was still talking with them, Rachel came with her father's sheep, for she was a shepherdess. When Jacob

saw Rachel daughter of Laban, his mother's brother, and Laban's sheep, he went over and rolled the stone away from the mouth of the well and watered his uncle's sheep. Then Jacob kissed Rachel and began to weep aloud. He had told Rachel that he was a relative of her father and a son of Rebekah. So she ran and told her father. As soon as Laban heard the news about Jacob, his sister's son, he hurried to meet him. He embraced him and kissed him and brought him to his home, and there Jacob told him all these things.

Then Laban said to him, "You are my own flesh and blood."

After Jacob had stayed with him for a whole month, Laban said to him, "Just because you are a relative of mine, should you work for me for nothing? Tell me what your wages should be."

Now Laban had two daughters; the name of the older was Leah, and the name of the younger was Rachel. Leah had weak eyes, but Rachel was lovely in form, and beautiful.

Jacob was in love with Rachel and said, "I'll work for you seven years in return for your younger daughter Rachel."

Laban said, "It's better that I give her to you than to some other man. Stay here with me."

So Jacob served seven years to get Rachel, but they seemed like only a few days to him because of his love for her. Then Jacob said to Laban, "Give me my wife. My time is completed, and I want to lie with her."

So Laban brought together all the people of the place and gave a feast. But when evening came, he took his daughter Leah and gave her to Jacob, and Jacob lay with her. And Laban gave his servant girl Zilpah to his daughter as her maidservant. When morning came, there was Leah!

So Jacob said to Laban, "What is this you have done to me? I served you for Rachel, didn't I? Why have you deceived me?"

Laban replied, "It is not our custom here to give the younger daughter in marriage before the older one. Finish this daughter's bridal week; then we will give you the younger one also, in return for another seven years of work."

And Jacob did so. He finished the week with Leah, and then Laban gave him his daughter Rachel to be his wife. Laban gave his servant girl Bilhah to his daughter Rachel as her maidservant. Jacob lay with Rachel also, and he loved Rachel more than Leah. And he worked for Laban another seven years.

When the Lord saw that Leah was not loved, he opened her womb, but Rachel was barren. Leah became pregnant and gave birth to a son. She named him Reuben, for she said, "It is because the Lord has seen my misery. Surely my husband will love me now."

She conceived again, and when she gave birth to a son she said, "Because the Lord heard that I am not loved, he gave me this one too." So she named him Simeon.

Again she conceived, and when she gave birth to a son she said, "Now at last my husband will become attached to me, because I have borne him three sons." So he was named Levi.

She conceived again, and when she gave birth to a son she said, "This time I will praise the Lord." So she named him Judah. Then she stopped having children.

There are several things to note from this passage. In God's way there is divine order. Jacob saw who he wanted. She caught his eye. She didn't take his card and call him. She didn't ask him out on a date. She didn't ask him to dance. She didn't buy tickets to a play and take him. She didn't take him out to dinner. She didn't work to get him. Jacob worked to have Rachel. She cost Jacob something.

Rachel was busy working when Jacob saw her. She was not looking all around for a man. She was not looking to see who was available. She was doing the work that was assigned to her.

Jacob approached Rachel. She allowed him to make the first move.

Jacob saw her and got so exited he was able to roll the stone away, which usually took several men to move. Rachel moved Jacob to do things he would not have ordinarily done. And he helped her in her mission as well. Jacob moved the stone away and watered the sheep she was shepherding. Often we have this backward. We want to do all we can for the man we are dating. That is not God's way. He shows us in this example. Jacob helped Rachel, and Rachel let him. As a woman, receive your blessings.

God gave Eve to Adam as a helpmate in marriage. Often we as women give men too much help when we are not married, and then we wonder why he doesn't marry us. Why marry you when you are doing so much for him now?

Rachel did not ask for Jacob's help. He gave it to her. A man will do for you what he wants to do. In the initial stages, let him offer what gifts he is willing to give. See what he does. See what is in his heart. Is there care and concern for you?

Jacob was so overjoyed with Rachel that he kissed her and began to weep aloud. He had an outward show of affection for her, and he was not afraid to let those around him see his feelings for Rachel. How does your man act when you are around his friends and family? How does he treat you around them? Does he only show his feelings for you when the two of you are alone?

Jacob stayed with and worked for Laban to be near Rachel for a month, without wages. A man wants the woman of his dreams in his presence. He wants to be around her and be near her.

Laban had a hand in who married his daughters. Why do you think he chose Jacob? Laban saw Jacob had worked for him for an entire month without pay. That's something you don't see every day, a man working for a month without receiving any money. And being the wise man he was, Laban saw Jacob's motivation for working for a month without pay. He saw that Jacob loved his daughter Rachel. It can be important to let your family members and friends meet the man you are dating. They may be able to see those good—and bad—characteristics you do not see.

When asked by Laban what he wanted for his labor, Jacob knew what he wanted. He wanted and he chose Rachel.

After being deceived by Laban, Jacob had sex with Leah but was calling for Rachel the next day. This should let women know that a man will sleep with you one night and in the morning be calling another woman's name. We like to think that because we are having sex with him and giving him "the precious" he will want us and no one else. *Not true.* If you are not his true love, he will take your precious and be going after the woman who has his heart in the next second. Don't fool yourself.

Jacob didn't want Leah, and no amount of sex was going to change that. Jacob offered to work and wait seven years to have Rachel. He was willing to pay the cost to have the lady he desired. What has your man done to prove his love for you? If he loves you, he will come and pick you up. He will pay for dinner if it's in his means. He will pay the cost to have the woman who holds his heart. And some men will say what their last girlfriends did for them, but you see what those girlfriends did wasn't enough to keep him, so just tell him you are going to do things God's way. You can even ask, "Well, if she did all of that, why aren't you still with her?"

## WHAT THREE THINGS DO YOU NEED IN A MAN?

Laban deceived Jacob and gave him Leah instead of Rachel on his wedding night. If you give yourself to a man and he didn't choose you, he may sleep with you but there's a good chance he will not love you. Are you his heart's desire or only someone for him to sleep with?

When the Lord saw Leah was not loved, he opened her womb and gave her a son. God sees our pains and frustrations. He provides us with the love we need. Leah wanted someone to love her, and God gave her someone, her son. That's how much our Father cares for us. He meets us at our needs. Your situation will change with God on your side.

The Lord saw Leah's misery. Leah was in a miserable situation. She was with a man who did not love her. That is a miserable situation to be in. Don't put yourself in this situation by being with a man who did not choose you. Did *you* approach *him?*

Leah felt that because she had bore Jacob a son he would love her, but he didn't. That kind of thinking still exists today. Some women think having a child by a man will cause him to love her. This is not how God ordained things to work, and He shows us in His Word that it won't work. God is always trying to help us, which is why He gives us these examples. We must be willing to accept the goodness of His ways for our lives, or we can accept the consequences of doing things our way.

Leah gave birth to three sons hoping Jacob would love her, but nothing changed. No amount of children will cause his heart to change either.

When Leah gave birth to the fourth son, she finally got the picture and praised God for the gifts He had given her. She was able to see the children for the gifts they were and be thankful. Those children were giving her the unconditional love she was not getting from Jacob. Has God given you unconditional love in the gift of children and you haven't realized what God has done and given Him the praise He deserves?

Leah conceived again, and when she gave birth to a son, she said, "This time I will praise the Lord," so she named him Judah. Then she stopped having children. Did she understand that no amount of children was going to make a man love her? Did she become content with her situation? Did she finally decide to accept the love that was offered to her from her children? Will you accept the love from the people who God has put in your life to love you?

The situation changed for Leah when she changed her focus from Jacob to God. Will you change your situation by changing your focus from a man to the Father?

You can't change the Jacobs of the world. Only God could change Jacob. According to Genesis 32:26, only when Jacob met God and wrestled with Him was he changed.

Are you a Leah or a Rachel?

The third characteristic you want to see in a man is love. You want a man who will love you. What does love look like?

First Corinthians 13:4–8a says,

> Love is patient, love is kind. It does not envy, it does not boast, it is not proud. It is not rude, it is not self-seeking, it is not easily angered, it keeps no record of wrongs. Love does not delight in evil but rejoices with the truth. It always protects, always trusts, always hopes, always perseveres.
>
> Love never fails.

Love is patient and kind. Love does not envy what someone else has. Love does not boast and brag about what it does have. The man you date should not try to impress you with the things he has. If you are impressed with objects instead of the man, then those things will be the object of your affection. The true nature of the man will be hidden behind the objects he is flaunting in front of you. See through the house and the car to the heart of the person.

Love is neither rude nor self-seeking. If he is rude to you, tell him about it and see if he straightens up and changes or you may have to let him go. Love considers what is best for the relationship. Love is not easily angered. It's okay for him to get angry, but if he gets angry about the smallest little things and he gets angry often, this is not love. He may be trying to control you with fear. Love does not bring up past wrongs but forgives and moves on. Love protects, trusts in God, hopes in God, and perseveres, knowing GOD IS ABLE. Love never fails.

# 12
## Resist The Devil And He Will Flee

There is a time when we should say "No." To resist Satan is to say no to sinful requests. For instance, if a guy asks me for sex and I say "No" and he leaves and never comes back, I thank my Father above. People with evil intentions will not be able to stand the light in us. God has designed it so that we may know what we are dealing with. By him leaving, I will know he was just there for sex. God is showing me what is in this person's heart.

Sometimes we chase men down after they leave us. After they flee, we go after them. God would not have us go after evil doers. God meant for the evil doer to flee. The Devil has left the building. Let him go.

Remember what your temptations are. Know what your weaknesses are. My weakness was that I would stop whatever I was doing and answer a call from Charles. I could be talking to my sister, who I hardly see and stays out of town, and he would call. I would tell her I would call her later. I would call Charles back immediately after I received a message from him. When I went to visit my family out of town, I would stay on the phone talking to him more than spending time with my family.

# MY TESTIMONY

The reason this was out of order is because I didn't make time for my Heavenly Father like I did for this man. I had it twisted. I was jumping to whatever Charles wanted. I was jumping whenever he called. I needed to stay aware of my shortcomings so I could be mindful, do better, and not revert to that behavior. I had to remember where I came from and what bad behavior had gotten me into trouble in the first place. I had to work on balance and resist going back to what I was use to. That takes time. It's a process, but it's a process that leads to liberation.

Galatians 4:8–9 says, "Formerly, when you did not know God, you were slaves to those who by nature are not gods. But now that you know God—or rather are known by God—how is it that you are turning back to those weak and miserable principles? Do you wish to be enslaved by them all over again?"

In order that we don't continue to make the same mistakes, the Bible gives us guidance. Jesus tells us that the examination should always start with us. Before we make a judgment about someone else, we should take a look to see if we are doing the same thing we are accusing someone else of doing. Jesus calls those people hypocrites. People in our lives serve as our reflection so we can see ourselves—the part of us we don't want to admit is us, the broken part that we are not dealing with.

I would call Antonio selfish. I would say our problems were because of him. After taking a good look at myself, I saw I was the same way. I was very selfish. I did things for someone else's approval or applause. My motivation for doing so many things wasn't for God's glory, it was for mine. I wanted to be recognized for my good works. The things I was finding fault in other people were the same things I did myself. For instance, I would complain about my sister fussing at her kids when I did the same thing. I would complain about someone cutting in too close between me and the car in front of me, and then I realized that's how I drive. When I would do those things, my spirit would say, "See? You do it too."

Matthew 7:1–5 says,

> "Do not judge, or you too will be judged. For in the same way you judge others, you will be judged, and with the measure you use, it will be measured to you.
>
> "Why do you look at the speck of sawdust in your brother's eye and pay no attention to the plank in your own eye? How can you say to your brother, 'Let me take the speck out of your eye,' when all the time there is a plank in your own eye? You hypocrite, first take the plank out of your own eye, and then you will see clearly to remove the speck from your brother's eye."

God wants us to live life to the fullest and will give us the understanding that we seek, but we must first seek the understanding. It's funny, I would wonder why something was a certain way, then I would find the answer in my Bible study or from a sermon or from someone's conversation. It would amaze me every time when God would reveal something to me. He would answer my questions. I would be like, wow! The more I sought answers from my Father, the more He revealed the answers to me. He opened my eyes so I could see. Matthew 7:7–8 assures us, "Ask and it will be given to you; seek and you will find; knock and the door will be opened to you. For everyone who asks receives; he who seeks finds; and to him who knocks, the door will be opened."

You can't always trust what a person says. Words are very manipulative. We must look to a person's actions to discern what is in their hearts. If you listen and observe their behavior, the truth will be revealed. Practice awareness. People will come in sheep's clothing so they will look harmless enough, but don't let the smile fool you. Don't let the greetings fool you. Don't let the pretty face fool you. Matthew 7:15–20 lets us know,

"Watch out for false prophets. They come to you in sheep's clothing, but inwardly they are ferocious wolves. By their fruit you will recognize them. Do people pick grapes from thornbushes, or figs from thistles? Likewise every good tree bears good fruit, but a bad tree bears bad fruit. A good tree cannot bear bad fruit, and a bad tree cannot bear good fruit. Every tree that does not bear good fruit is cut down and thrown into the fire. Thus, by their fruit you will recognize them."

Sometimes after we sin, we want to hide from God, as did our ancestors, Adam and Eve. We stop going to church because we know what we are doing is wrong, but God still sees us and is trying to get our attention. God loves us no matter what we do. He loves us but hates the sin. He is still calling out to you, "Where are you?" Go ahead and tell Him what you have done wrong. He knows already. We can't hide from an all-knowing God. He is the God of another chance.

Genesis 3:8–9 says, "Then the man and his wife heard the sound of the Lord God as he was walking in the garden in the cool of the day, and they hid from the Lord God among the trees of the garden. But the Lord God called to the man, 'Where are you?'"

God asks, "Have you disobeyed me?" He is asking you now. In what way have you been disobedient? Tell God about it without blaming the man you dated, or your mother for not instructing you in a better way, or your uncle for abusing you. Just say, "Yes, Lord, this is how I was disobedient."

Genesis 3:11–12 says, "And he said, 'Who told you that you were naked? Have you eaten from the tree that I commanded you not to eat from?' The man said, 'The woman you put here with me—she gave me some fruit from the tree, and I ate it.'" We are to be aware when we blame others for doing things God has commanded us not to do.

God punishes us for our sins. He disciplines us so we can remember not to commit that sin again. Discipline is there to show us if we choose obedience, we choose life. If we choose disobedience, we choose the consequences associated with it. God punishes us to make us better.

Genesis 3:21 tells us that God made garments of skin for Adam and his wife and clothed them. God still loved them and made provisions for them and showed them grace and mercy. He gave them another chance. God will give you another chance as well. *That's* good news!

# 13

## What Does A Man Of GOD Look Like?

God wants us women to know we are to respond to a man's show of affection. We are to respond to evidence of caring and protection, and desire not his words only. God gives us the beautiful example of how Boaz provides for, shows interest in, and cares for Ruth. Naomi, Ruth's mother-in-law, knows Boaz is doing the things he does for a reason. Naomi is able to see what is in Boaz's heart based on what he has done for Ruth. Ruth's husband had passed away and instead of going back to her father's house, she moved to Bethlehem with Naomi.

Ruth decided to go to the fields to work to support herself and her mother-in-law. As it turned out, she found herself working in a field that belonged to Boaz, a relative of Naomi. Boaz noticed Ruth and instructed her not to go away from his field to work. He reasoned she might get hurt in someone else's field. He also instructed his men not to harm Ruth.

At mealtime, Boaz fed her. Then, in order that Ruth would have enough grain, Boaz instructed his men to leave some stalks for her to pick up.

Naomi wanted Ruth to have a husband who would take care of her. Naomi instructed Ruth to get dressed and go to the threshing room floor where Boaz was. After Boaz realized that Ruth had responded to his advances, he headed into town to settle Naomi's estate and make Ruth his wife.

I have included the characteristics of Ruth, Naomi, and Boaz to give us insight on what a godly man looks like. We can compare the characteristics of Boaz to the men in our lives and see how they match up. We can also teach Boaz's qualities to our sons so they will know what their responsibilities are as far as being in a relationship with the woman they want to marry.

I would like to encourage you to read the entire book of Ruth. Ruth is also a wonderful example for the woman who has been previously married. She shows all women what to do when the man in our lives is no longer there. After her husband's death, Ruth focused on providing and caring for herself and those God had placed in her life, namely, her mother-in-law. We could learn a lot from this godly woman, Ruth.

Characteristics of Ruth

1. Ruth, chapter 1, illustrates the closeness of Naomi and Ruth's relationship. It is good to have helpful, loving, female relationships. We can learn from the wisdom of older, more experienced women. They have knowledge we do not have. It would do us good to listen to them. Listen to what Ruth tells Naomi 1:16–17: "But Ruth replied, 'Don't urge me to leave you or to turn back from you. Where you go, I will go, and where you stay I will stay. Your people will be my people and your God my God. Where you die I will die, and there I will be buried. May the Lord deal with me, be it ever so severely, if anything but death separates you and me.'"

2. Ruth 2:2 shows us that Ruth was willing to work and provide for herself and her mother-in-law. Ruth cared about someone besides herself and was willing to work and support this older lady in her life. "And Ruth the Moabitess said to Naomi, 'Let me go to the fields and pick up the leftover grain behind anyone in whose eyes I find favor.'" Ruth was not looking for some man to provide for her. She was an independent woman who could work and provide for herself.

3. Ruth 2:10 shows us how thankful Ruth was for Boaz's provisions. She saw his goodness. Have you overlooked the goodness of a man in your life? Have you thanked him for his kindness? Ruth accepted and was thankful for the instructions Boaz had given her that would benefit her life. Boaz's instructions were evidence that he cared for her. "At this, she bowed down with her face to the ground. She exclaimed, 'Why have I found such favor in your eyes that you notice me—a foreigner?'"

4. Ruth 2:14 shows us that Ruth was willing to let Boaz feed her. She accepted his provisions for her and her mother-in-law. "At mealtime Boaz said to her, 'Come over here. Have some bread and dip it in the wine vinegar.' When she sat down with the harvesters, he offered her some roasted grain. She ate all she wanted and had some left over."

5. Ruth 2:17–18 tells us that Ruth was thoughtful and shared what she had with her mother-in-law. Some women reading this book are mothers-in-law, or will be. This passage shows the importance of your relationship to your daughter-in-law. Often, mothers-in-law don't get the blessing God has for them because of the nasty way

they treat their daughters-in-law.

6. In reading the account of Ruth, we see that because of these two women's closeness, Naomi was blessed when Ruth was blessed. Boaz provided for Ruth, and Ruth, in return, shared with Naomi. When Ruth had a son, we learn the baby was a joyful part of Naomi's life. The baby gave Naomi something to live for after all the loss she had experienced. This blessing happened to her because she had a loving relationship with her daughter-in-law.

7. "So Ruth gleaned in the field until evening. Then she threshed the barley she had gathered, and it amounted to about an ephah. She carried it back to town, and her mother-in-law saw how much she had gathered. Ruth also brought out and gave her what she had left over after she had eaten enough."

Characteristics of Naomi

1. Ruth 2:19 shows that Naomi was wise enough to know a blessing in the form of a good man when she saw one. Naomi was aware of how much Boaz had supported and protected Ruth. "Her mother-in-law asked her, 'Where did you glean today? Where did you work? Blessed be the man who took notice of you!' Then Ruth told her mother-in-law about the one at whose place she had been working. 'The name of the man I worked with today is Boaz,' she said."

2. In Ruth 3:1–4, Naomi gave Ruth instructions on how to handle the situation with Boaz. Naomi was wise enough to encourage Ruth to let Boaz know she was interested in him. When Naomi instructed Ruth to go and lay down at Boaz's feet, she was insuring that Ruth responded to

the love shown to her by Boaz. The man had done these things for Ruth for a reason. Naomi was wise enough to see Boaz's love for Ruth and instructed Ruth to respond to his obvious care.

3. We are taught in Second Corinthians 6:11–13 how we should receive love: "We have spoken freely to you, Corinthians, and opened wide our hearts to you. We are not withholding our affection from you, but you are withholding yours from us. As a fair exchange—I speak as to my children—open wide your hearts also." Sometimes we don't have love relationships in our lives because we reject good men.

The Bible gives women an example of what a man who cares for you looks like. This example is here to teach you how to know what is in a man's heart because we will see what's in his heart based on his actions. What do we see in Boaz?

Characteristics of Boaz

1. Ruth 2:3 shows us Boaz owned a field and he had a job. "… As it turned out, she found herself working in a field belonging to Boaz …"

2. Ruth 2:5 tells us that Boaz inquired about Ruth. He wanted to find out what he could about her. When a man is interested in a woman, he asks questions about her. What will a man find out when he asks about you? Your reputation precedes you. "Boaz asked the foreman of his harvesters, 'Whose young woman is that?'"

3. Ruth 2:8–9 shows us how Boaz protected Ruth. He told her not to go to another field, and he told the men who worked for him not to touch her. Boaz told her if she got thirsty, take some of his water. How has your man shown you he wants

what is best for you? Are his instructions going to bless you? Is he looking out for your best interests? Godly men provide and protect. "So Boaz said to Ruth, 'My daughter, listen to me. Don't go and glean in another field and don't go away from here. Stay here with my servant girls. Watch the field where the men are harvesting, and follow along after the girls. I have told the men not to touch you. And whenever you are thirsty, go and get a drink from the water jars the men have filled.'"

4. Ruth 2:14 shows us Boaz fed Ruth. She didn't feed him. He fed her. He made sure her basic needs were met. This is how it should be. She may cook for him later, but he makes the first gesture. "At mealtime Boaz said to her, 'Come over here. Have some bread and dip it in the water vinegar.'"

5. Ruth 2:15–16 tells us Boaz provided for Ruth through others. He told his men not to embarrass her and to leave some stalks for her to pick up. Boaz's arm of protection extended to the people who were around Ruth. He dealt with them in order that she would be protected. "As she got up to glean, Boaz gave orders to his men, 'Even if she gathers among the sheaves, don't embarrass her. Rather, pull out some stalks for her from the bundles and leave them for her to pick up, and don't rebuke her.'"

6. Ruth 4:1–12 shows us Boaz was a man of honesty and integrity in his dealings. Will the man in your life do what is right, or does he do what is easy and convenient for him, regardless of the law?

7. Ruth 4:13 tells us that Boaz married Ruth. Boaz knew the characteristics he wanted in a wife. He saw Ruth's care-giving, hardworking qualities. After showing Ruth that he cared for her and after her response, Boaz didn't wait years to settle

the matter that was in his heart. He made the woman he cared for his wife. He wanted all of her. Where there is love, there is no doubt.

Wait on your Boaz, ladies. God put Ruth in the right place at the right time to receive her blessing. *God will provide.*

# 14

# Not Guilty

Once I shared my testimony and elaborated on how I had slept with a married man. The person I was talking to said she was glad she had never done that before. I told her I was glad she hadn't either. It was a horrible thing. I say this because people want to put weight on one sin versus another.

We have all sinned and come short of the glory of God. James 2:10 tells us, "For whoever keeps the whole law and yet stumbles at just one point is guilty of breaking all of it." If you have committed one sin, you have broken the law. Why? Because all sins are wrong in God's sight, and they all require confession, repentance, and a faith walk of obedience. No matter what you have done that someone else hasn't, if you confess and ask for forgiveness, God will surely forgive. Your sins will be washed away, and you will become as white as snow.

*Not guilty.* In John 8:7 (KJV), Jesus told the people who brought the woman to him who was caught in adultery and who was to be stoned, "He that is without sin among you, let him first cast a stone at her." If someone wants to judge what you have done, you can say, "The one without sin cast the first stone." In other words,

# MY TESTIMONY

"So, you've never done *anything* wrong?" Who the Son sets free is free indeed (John 8:36). If you are walking in God's freedom, don't allow someone's comments to condemn you. No matter if you have killed someone, slept with you sister's husband, mistreated your parents, been addicted to drugs, it doesn't matter. Come to God as you are.

Could you ever imagine that perhaps the sickness you are going through is going to give God glory? Jesus knew Lazarus, Mary's brother, was sick (John 11:1–44). He purposefully waited to go to him. Why would Jesus not immediately rush back to his friend and heal him? Because Jesus wanted everyone to see the glory of God. This was to be a testimony that God healed Lazarus. "So the sisters sent word to Jesus, 'Lord, the one you love is sick.' When he heard this, Jesus said, 'This sickness will not end in death. No, it is for God's glory so that God's Son may be glorified through it (John 11:3–4).'"

Trials happen for God's glory to be revealed. It happens so you can see how much He loves you after He heals you. It is so you will believe. John 11:14–15, "So then he told them plainly, 'Lazarus is dead, And for your sake I am glad I was not there, so that you may believe. But let us go to him.'" According to John 11:43–44, "When he had said this, Jesus called in a loud voice, 'Lazarus, come out!' The dead man came out, his hands and feet wrapped with strips of linen, and a cloth around his face."

The sickness I was experiencing would not end in death. God had other plans. He would get the glory through my testimony in this book. You see, my tears moved Jesus. He heard my cry.

Have you ever felt like you wanted to die because of a relationship? Has a relationship ever had you depressed? Well, there is hope. There is healing. Just know you will rise again. You will rise from your depression. You will rise from the death of a relationship. Jesus is the resurrection and the life. Do you believe He can restore you? All you have to do is tell God your situation and ask Him to help you. Then just watch. He will make a believer out of you, and you will see the glory of God. He will give you life after a death experience. The glory of God will give you peace that surpasses all understanding. The glory of God will give you a new walk and a new talk and a new confidence.

Inviting Jesus into your situation will change things for the better. What are you suffering from? Low self-esteem? Loneliness? Overeating? Fear of what others think? Debt? Abuse?

There is help. Mark 5:24–34 tells us,

> So Jesus went with him. A large crowd followed and pressed around him. And a woman was there who had been subject to bleeding for twelve years. She had suffered a great deal under the care of many doctors and had spent all she had, yet instead of getting better she grew worse.
>
> When she heard about Jesus, she came up behind him in the crowd and touched his cloak, because she thought, "If I just touch his clothes, I will be healed." Immediately her bleeding stopped and she felt in her body that she was freed from her suffering. At once Jesus realized that power had gone out from him. He turned around in the crowd and asked, "Who touched my clothes?"
>
> "You see the people crowding against you," his disciples answered, "and yet you can ask, 'Who touched me?'"
>
> But Jesus kept looking around to see who had done it. Then the woman, knowing what had happened to her, came and fell at his feet and, trembling with fear, told him the whole truth.
>
> He said to her, "Daughter, your faith has healed you. Go

in peace and be freed from your suffering."

The scripture explains that this nameless woman had been suffering for twelve years. She had sought help from many doctors, but she continued to get worse. Have you sought help from friends, doctors, counselors, parents, pastors, and yet, your situation just keeps getting worse?

You have tried it your way, the doctor's way, and your boyfriend's way. It is now time to seek Jesus. The woman said if she could just touch His clothes, she would be healed. She thought, *I will try Jesus*. What did she have to lose? She was out of money.

After touching Jesus' garment, she immediately stopped bleeding and was freed from her suffering. She sought Jesus, and she wasn't going to let anyone get in her way. She believed He could heal her, and He did. What do *you* believe? You can try Jesus last or you can try Him first. It's your choice.

Jesus explained to the woman that her faith in Him as a healer healed her and she could go in peace and be free from her suffering. Do you want to be free from your suffering? Turn to Jesus. Seek Him. He is willing to heal you. Don't allow your family or friends to get in the way of your healing. Press your way to Jesus. Jesus is the Doctor who has never lost a patient.

We have all participated in destructive behaviors before knowing Christ. The Apostle Paul writes to the church at Philippians of his destructive ways before he came to know Christ for himself. If we are honest, we can admit we all have been there. We have all had destructive behaviors before our knowledge of Christ. Philippians 3:1–11 says,

> Finally, my brothers, rejoice in the Lord! It is no trouble for me to write the same things to you again, and it is a safeguard for you.

Watch out for those dogs, those men who do evil, those mutilators of the flesh. For it is we who are the circumcision, we who worship by the Spirit of God, who glory in Christ Jesus, and who put no confidence in the flesh—though I myself have reasons for such confidence.

If anyone else thinks he has reasons to put confidence in the flesh, I have more: Circumcised on the eighth day, of the people of Israel, of the tribe of Benjamin, a Hebrew of Hebrews; in regard to the law, a Pharisee; as for zeal, persecuting the church; as for legalistic righteousness, faultless.

But whatever was to my profit I now consider loss for the sake of Christ. What is more, I consider everything a loss compared to the surpassing greatness of knowing Christ Jesus my Lord, for whose sake I have lost all things. I consider them rubbish, that I may gain Christ and be found in him, not having a righteousness of my own that comes from the law, but that which is through faith in Christ—the righteousness that comes from God and is by faith. I want to know Christ and the power of his resurrection and the fellowship of sharing in his sufferings, becoming like him in his death, and so, somehow, to attain to the resurrection from the dead.

Paul points out his position in society. He was a descendent from the house of Benjamin. He was a Hebrew, considered the religious people of the times. He was well versed in the law so he was considered a Pharisee, a teacher with knowledge. And he was considered faultless because of his legalistic righteousness, which means he was righteous by the world's standards—not by God's standards.

But with all he had going for him, Paul was greatly mistaken in his walk. He had conformed to the world at the time and had worldly views. We have all been there. We got a man by the world's standards and was having sex with him and was thinking we had the life. We may have thought nothing of our fornication. We may have thought we were right with what we were doing. We had a big house, nice clothes, and thought everything was fine. We had it going on with our careers, and by the world's standards, we were on top. We enjoyed vacationing and buying what we wanted when we wanted it, but it never satisfied us. We were never satisfied with all of the status, money, relationships, cars, homes, and wealth.

Legalistic righteousness tells us it is okay to have sex before marriage—everybody else is doing it. Legalistic righteousness tells us it's okay to date someone else's husband, to take something that doesn't belong to you without asking, to live outside your means and be in debt, to gossip and judge others. Lord, help us to know You and Your ways. The yardstick that we must use in life is not the worldly view, but God's teachings.

Even our going to church on Sundays and singing in the choir and teaching a Bible study class is only legalistic righteousness if we do not know Jesus. If we do not know Him, it's all for show. The scripture tells us doing these things are for our profit if we do not know Him. It is religion without relationship. We must have a relationship with the Father. We must grow deeper in our knowledge of Him.

Whatever you have gained has been worthless until you know Jesus. All of it is for show until you know Christ. We do so many things out of habit or because others are doing them. Oh, to know Him. You can count it all loss for the sake of Christ.

What is keeping you from a closer walk with Jesus? What will you have to lose before you decide for yourself to seek Him? Will you get AIDS? Go to jail? Lose your house? Car? Boyfriend? A body part? A job? What is it going to take to get your attention?

You may have to lose some things to bring you closer to the Father. Count it all joy because only in Him will you find fulfillment. Knowing Him is liberation.

What will you give up so you can get to know Him? Will you turn off your television and spend time in His Word? Will you stop doing some of the busy things you are doing to find time for the Lord? We make time for what we want to do. Will we make time or will our choices and their consequences put us in a position where we have nothing left but God? Either way, it is His purpose that you might know Christ Jesus. Our rightness with God comes from knowing His son and having faith in Him. John 14:6 Jesus answered, "I am the way and the truth and the life. No one comes to the Father except through me."

There is power in the resurrection of Jesus. The same power that lifted Him up can lift you up out of the situation and turmoil you are experiencing. Is your life all that it could be? Knowing Christ is the answer for you. Don't try to fix someone else. The lesson is for you. Then, with your testimony of what God has done for you, you can go and help your brother.

We have all suffered, and if you haven't, keep living. The fellowship of the suffering is to show you that you are in God's family, and we all suffer so we can see what God can, and will, do for us if we let Him. How can you see His power and love in your life if you don't witness for yourself His healing, resurrecting power? You can be resurrected from your dead state of living by knowing Christ Jesus for yourself.

# 15

## A Lesson On Competition

Why do we feel the need to compete with other women? Have we been told there are only a few good men out there? Do we feel a need to cook the best dinner, wear the most revealing clothes, clean his house, and buy him nice things so he will stay with us?

We are to run the race God has set before us. The competition should be with ourselves, not with the person next to us. We should strive to be the best we can be. God has given us all different talents and skills. The person you think is your competition may be better in one area and you may be better in another. Instead of fighting against her, help her be the best she can be. This is what Christ would have us do. Love your neighbor as yourself.

Antonio and I were at a nightclub in Arlington. I saw him eyeing a beautiful lady. Then I saw her look at him and smile. I looked at her and said, "If you want him, you can have him." I realized the jewel I am, and if he wanted her or anyone else—his loss. I was not going to fight her or make a scene. I said that, and I was through.

Once when I was taking a beginner's sewing class, I was getting my pajama bottoms finished and it was time to iron the seam. One of the ladies in the class rushed to the ironing board to get there before me. I slowed down and took extra time to get to the iron. I was telling her that she could have it. I wasn't in competition with her. I was working at my own pace.

Then there was this time I was at a Christmas party and there were items out for a silent auction. A lady was bidding on the same painting I was bidding on. She put down a bid and said to me, "Now what are you going to do?" I put in my bid and walked away. My bid had nothing to do with her. I was not outbidding her. I knew what the painting was worth to me, and no more. She paid five dollars more than I had bid and got the painting. I wasn't going to allow what she was doing affect my decision. This should be our mind-set in dating. What some other woman is doing does not dictate what we are going to do.

You are God's masterpiece. So often we live below the standard God has set for us because we think if we love ourselves and are confident, then we are conceited and vain. There is a difference. Remember, Scripture calls us to love ourselves.

To be conceited is to think of yourself as being more than others. To love yourself is a commandment. It is to take care of yourself—your mental, physical, spiritual, and financial well-being. We are to love our neighbors in this same light. Love is growth.

It is okay to look in the mirror and like what you see. Vanity is spending most of the day in the mirror admiring yourself. It is all about the looks. Your looks make you; they break you. To be confident in who God has made you is to accept your inner being—your spirit as well as your outward appearance. You are confident in God's handiwork. You are confident is His details. You are His masterpiece, and you are proud of that.

I was reading in Exodus where it talks about the Tabernacle, the Ark, the Lampstand, the Altar of Incense, the Altar of Burnt Offering, the Basin for Washing, the Courtyard, and the Priestly

## A LESSON ON COMPETITION

Garments—all the things the Israelites made in order to worship God. I was telling my brother how I was so ready to get back to the "juicy" stuff, like where God killed Judah's sons because they were wicked.

There were just so many details to the building of each of these items. Chapter after chapter was laid out with every measurement and how precisely the items were to be put together. I told my brother God must have meant for men to enjoy all of this information about the details of building things and putting them together. Then my brother said, "God is into details."

That wowed me. *God is into the details.* He is all about specifics.

Some time later as I was driving (which is when I hear God's voice quite often), He said to me, "I am into the details of your very being. You are My masterpiece." Glory to God! I ran with that. God is in the details of everything about me. He is in the details of my eyes, my nose, my skin color, my toes, my hips, my lips, my elbows. When you see me, you see Him. I am His essence. I am His masterpiece. You are His masterpiece. He is in your details. He is in the specifics of your design.

It's like when you see a magnificent sunset or a beautiful flower and you say, "Look at God." Take a minute and look in the mirror and say, "Look at God." There is reason to have confidence. There is reason to be proud of God's creation: YOU.

# 16

## To Be Treated Like A Lady, Act Like One

When we desire to be married, there are certain things we must understand. In a relationship, the man takes charge. He proposes. Biologically, he's the aggressor. A lady understands the natural order of the universe: the man pursues the woman. He makes things happen. The man must take the lead. Proverbs 18:22 (KJV) says, "Whoso findeth a wife findeth a good thing, and obtaineth favour of the Lord." It's God's plan for our husbands to find us.

Second Samuel 11:2–4 tells us,

> "One evening David got up from his bed and walked around on the roof of the palace. From the roof he saw a woman bathing. The woman was very beautiful, and David sent someone to find out about her. The man said, 'Isn't this Bathsheba, the daughter of Eliam and the wife of Uriah the Hittite?' Then David sent messengers to get her. She came to him, and he slept with her. (She had purified herself from her uncleanness.) Then she went back home.

Second Samuel 11:14–15, continues, "In the morning David

wrote a letter to Joab and sent it with Uriah. In it he wrote, 'Put Uriah in the front line where the fighting is fiercest. Then withdraw from him so he will be struck down and die.'"

Second Samuel 11:26–27 finishes with, "When Uriah's wife heard that her husband was dead, she mourned for him. After the time of mourning was over, David had her brought to his house, and she became his wife and bore him a son. But the thing David had done displeased the Lord."

By reading this passage, what does it say about David?

This chapter in the book of Samuel tells us that King David saw who he wanted and went after her. When Bathsheba became pregnant by David, he tried to cover the pregnancy up by having her husband come home from battle and sleep with her. When that didn't work, David got Uriah drunk, thinking he would go home and sleep with his wife. When that didn't work, David devised a way for Uriah to be killed in battle. After Uriah was killed, David took Bathsheba as his wife.

I'm not suggesting someone kill someone to have you. I am using this example to show that a man goes after who he wants and he lets very little stand in his way. If a man doesn't bother to walk across the room to seek you out and ask for your number, then he's obviously not interested enough, and asking him for his number won't change his feelings—or rather *lack* of feelings—for you. He'll probably be flattered you asked and give you the digits to be polite, and he might even have sex with you, but he won't be crazy about you. He never got the chance to pursue you, and this fact will always pervade the relationship.

Don't try to figure out why someone hasn't asked you out or approached you. There is always a good reason. The man may be married, dating someone, or just not interested. Know for yourself that if not him, then there's someone better.

God is still keeping men from sinning against Him by not letting them touch us. He is staying their hands. When we wonder why someone didn't call or come by, it may be because God has put a stop to the contact because He has plans for you to be someone else's wife. God knows. He has the big picture. God doesn't want that man to touch you. You belong to someone else. You can thank God for His love for you.

This is the account of how God would not let a man touch Sarah because God had not given Sarah to this man but to someone else. He does the same thing for us. Genesis 20:1–7 says,

> Now Abraham moved on from there into the region of the Negev and lived between Kadesh and Shur. For a while he stayed in Gerar, and there Abraham said of his wife Sarah, "She is my sister." Then Abimelech king of Gerar sent for Sarah and took her.
>
> But God came to Abimelech in a dream one night and said to him, "You are as good as dead because of the woman you have taken; she is a married woman."
>
> Now Abimelech had not gone near her, so he said, "Lord, will you destroy an innocent nation? Did he not say to me, 'She is my sister,' and didn't she also say, 'He is my brother'? I have done this with a clear conscience and clean hands."
>
> Then God said to him in the dream, "Yes, I know you did this with a clear conscience, and so I have kept you from sinning against me. That is why I did not let you touch her. Now return the man's wife, for he is a prophet, and he will pray for you and you will live. But if you do not return her, you may be sure that you and all yours will die."

When we don't get chosen by a certain man or he doesn't

continue to pursue us, we can choose to thank our Heavenly Father. He knows the plans He has for us. That man is the wrong man. That relationship was not meant to be. Understanding this truth can save you from many hurtful feelings because a certain man did not make a move on you or doesn't call after the first meeting. It's all in how you look at it.

Not only does the man choose the woman, but anytime a woman chases a man, he runs.

Genesis 39:6b–13 says,

> Now Joseph was well-built and handsome, and after a while his master's wife took notice of Joseph and said, "Come to bed with me!"
>
> But he refused. "With me in charge," he told her, "my master does not concern himself with anything in the house; everything he owns he has entrusted to my care. No one is greater in this house than I am. My master withheld nothing from me except you, because you are his wife. How then could I do such a wicked thing and sin against God?" And though she spoke to Joseph day after day, he refused to go to bed with her or even be with her.
>
> One day he went into the house to attend to his duties, and none of the household servants were inside. She caught him by his cloak and said, "Come to bed with me!" But he left his cloak in her hand and ran out of the house."

We see here Pharaoh's wife offered herself to Joseph. She chased after him. When a woman chases a man, he runs. God never intended for women to chase men. Now, a man may sleep with you since you are offering, but since you were not his choice, you will be forever chasing him. He will be with you because of what you are giving him. But as soon as the gifts are gone or he has had enough of you or someone else catches his eye, he is gone.

A man is an adult male, a piercer, an initiator, one who advances toward the horizon. A lady understands that the man is the initiator of the relationship. She doesn't talk to him first. When a woman goes against nature and talks to a man first, she interferes with whatever was supposed to happen or not happen. There is a big likelihood she will get hurt from causing a conversation or date to occur that was not meant to happen. Soon, like nature intended, he will pursue the girl who he is interested in. And the lady who pursued him will be left wondering what happened. Men know what they want.

We see with David and Jacob that a man will pursue the woman. Do you not believe the Scripture that says a man who finds a wife finds a good thing? A woman should not ask him out. He will make the move he wants to make. He is to initiate the process. If a woman initiates the relationship, then she will always be the initiator. She will wonder why he doesn't make plans for them and why he doesn't call. It will be because their relationship started from her initiating, and it will remain that way.

We also see that Pharaoh's wife chased after Joseph and he ran. We see that Leah slept with Jacob and that wasn't enough to make him want her. God is trying to stop the hurt. He wants to stop the tears, but we have got to get His way in our minds and in our hearts and in our actions. We must breathe in His teachings.

A man is attracted to a woman who displays wisdom and insight. She has her own set of standards and values in which she believes, and regardless of what he says or does, she holds fast to her beliefs. She is not swayed by what the man is telling her. She is not tossed and driven by the cares and worries of what he is up to. She is firmly grounded, which makes her simply irresistible. He has to have her. She possesses a certain self-confidence that distinguishes her from other women. She understands she is one-of-a-kind and that sense of confidence radiates her being from head to toe. She can take the man or leave him—which makes her very attractive.

We can ease our date's anxiety by avoiding staring romantically into his eyes. Otherwise, he will know you're already planning the honeymoon. Instead, look at the wall decoration or your food, or simply survey the crowd. It's best to seem generally interested in life, in others, in your surroundings, in the paintings, as opposed to your date. He may feel crowded and self-conscious if you stare at him too much. Men like other male species like to gain the female's attention and interest. A man wants to date a woman where there is no pressure that by this time next year, you two will be married.

A lady ends the date first. By ending the date first, it is likely she goes home at a decent hour. She leaves her date wanting more of her. We all remember the story of Cinderella, who got dressed and went to the ball. Her fairy godmother was a wise woman and told her to be home at a decent hour. Cinderella knew at a certain time that night she had to be heading home.

The prince took notice of Cinderella. After spending some time with him, Cinderella cut off their time together and went home. What did he do the next day? The prince searched throughout the land to get the lady of his dreams. We could learn a lot from Cinderella. As ladies, we should end things first, which allows our Prince Charming to come after us. We end the date, the phone call, holding his hand, and looking at him first. We are first to let go so that he can come closer.

A lady understands that a woman is an adult female, a pierced one, and the responsive one. She responds to a man's approaches. She responds to his pursuit. A lady allows a man to call her, and she returns his calls. To call a man first is to pursue him.

Ladies know to pace themselves in relationships. We are to enjoy our conversations with the man we are getting to know, but we practice limiting our conversations and not staying on the phone too long. Understand, talking to your date hours on end makes you transparent very quickly and runs the risk of making him tired and bored.

By getting off the phone first, you don't have to wonder if you've kept him on too long, bored him, or revealed too much about yourself. You don't make it seem as if you are waiting for him to ask you out. You have a life and aren't waiting on him to give you one. You can let him go instead of holding on. It is obvious to men when we prolong a call or a date. They can sense we need them or desire them deeply. You can get off the phone and go on with your life, no problem. This behavior allows you to have something to talk about the next time because you haven't said everything by being on the phone for hours. We've all been there—talked so much that there's nothing left to say for the next time.

It doesn't matter if you are having a great conversation and you want to tell him all about what happened at work. After forty minutes or so, it's time to go and continue the conversation some other time. This allows him to desire to talk to you again. It's like eating your favorite thing. If you consume the entire cake at once instead of a slice, you feel sick and tired of it and you can go a long time without having any again. Spending time with and talking to men is like your favorite food. If he ingests too much of you, he will want to go without you for a while to get over the massive amount he has taken in. We understand talking too much can be damaging to the relationship. So pace yourself.

By spending less time on the phone, it makes your man want to spend more time with you. He longs for you. Isn't that what we want—a man who longs for us? Sometimes days should pass before you talk to him. This intensifies the longing. It's okay if he gets upset because he couldn't reach you. First, you aren't married. He hasn't put a ring on your finger, so he has no claim to talk to you every day as if you were married. Second, it means he cares about you.

Also, getting off the phone shows him you have a full life and you are independent. You are a fulfilled, stable, functional, and happy person with a career, friends, and hobbies, and you are perfectly capable of living with or without him. You are not an empty vessel waiting for him to fill you up, support you, or give you a life. You are alive and enthusiastic, engaged in work and in living fully on your own.

I limited my phone calls with Kirk and Danny. Kirk complained about the lack of times I called him, and Danny would say things like, "I think about you all the time." Danny was able to think about me because he wasn't getting "Arquila overload."

A lady gives a man his space. She is okay if he wants to spend time with his friends playing golf, watching a game, or fishing. She is okay with him spending time with his children. She knows God would want him to spend time with his children and that there is enough love for her as well as them.

The man has to ask for a date without your help. Men will beat around the bush with asking you out. The guy you're interested in might say he has the weekend open, so you say you are available Saturday evening. His reply is Saturday evening doesn't work for him, so you say what about Sunday evening.

Two things just happened: First, he said he had the weekend opened and lied because now he is saying that Saturday doesn't work. Second, you are now asking him what date works for *his* schedule. You are coming up with a date and time instead of him. You are seeing if the date works for his schedule instead of him asking you if his plans work with *your* schedule. You are pursuing.

## TO BE TREATED LIKE A LADY, ACT LIKE ONE

It's important the man chases you without you offering ways of being caught. Let him figure it out and he will. Just know that often men have been spoiled by women who have made it easy to get a date with them. Being an easy catch might have been your behavior. It's never too late to be taught a better way.

A lady does not confuse her value with her valuables. She does not define her worth by the clothes she wears, the car she drives, the house she lives in, or her bank account. You are God's special flower, regardless of your possessions.

A lady tries to not use foul language. She understands the consequences of having a dirty mouth. A dirty mouth makes her very unattractive.

A lady creates her own happiness. Her man is just an added plus.

A lady dresses modestly so she does not cause men to stumble. She trains her thought life not to lust after men. First Corinthians 10:31–33 (brackets added) says, "So whether you eat or drink or whatever you do [whatever you wear], do it all for the glory of God. Do not cause anyone to stumble, whether Jews, Greeks [a man] or the church of God—even as I try to please everybody in every way. For I am not seeking my own good but the good of many, so that they may be saved."

A lady understands that it is okay to know a man's purpose for wanting to get to know her. Isaac sent his servant out to find him a wife. There was purpose. Jacob was on a mission to find a wife. He knew what he was looking for. As women, it is okay for us to discuss with the man we are dating which direction he is headed. Does he want to get to know us for the sake of considering marriage, or is his intent just to date with no direction or purpose?

A lady guards her heart by not engaging in premature interactions with men without clear direction as to the purpose of the relationship. Some things you just don't do until there is reason to. Proverbs 4:23 says, "Above all else, guard your heart, for it is the wellspring of life." Rebekah understood Isaac's intentions for their relationship. Genesis 24:63–67 says,

> He went out to the field one evening to meditate, and as he looked up, he saw camels approaching. Rebekah also looked up and saw Isaac. She got down from her camel and asked the servant, "Who is that man in the field coming to meet us?"
>
> "He is my master," the servant answered. So she took her veil and covered herself.
>
> Then the servant told Isaac all he had done. Isaac brought her into the tent of his mother Sarah, and he married Rebekah. So she became his wife, and he loved her; and Isaac was comforted after his mother's death.

In this passage, Abraham had sent his servant to get a wife for his son Isaac. We learn several things. First, Isaac saw Rebekah, and he approached her. Second, when Rebekah saw Isaac approaching, she let Isaac come to her. She stopped her forward progression. Third, she got down from her camel and covered up with her veil. It would do some of us good to cover up.

And after hearing what the servant had done, Isaac married Rebekah. God had answered the servant's prayer and given him a sign that Rebekah was the one. Isaac knew what he wanted. He wasn't dating other women. He didn't date her for years. Isaac met Rebekah, heard how the Lord had given his servant a sign of who to choose, took her into his mother's tent, and married her, and loved her. Men know what they want. They just want to see how much you are willing to give without him being committed to you. We should give very little.

So whether you experience a waiting period, like Jacob and Rachel, or things move quickly, like in the relationship of Isaac and Rebekah, let God help you make the right decision.

Also in dating, a lady understands that physical, emotional, and spiritual oneness, or the pursuit of it, is inappropriate with a man to whom she is not married. Ephesians 5:6–14 says,

> Let no one deceive you with empty words, for because of such things God's wrath comes on those who are disobedient. Therefore do not be partners with them.
>
> For you were once darkness, but now you are light in the Lord. Live as children of light (for the fruit of the light consists in all goodness, righteousness and truth) and find out what pleases the Lord. Have nothing to do with the fruitless deeds of darkness, but rather expose them. For it is shameful even to mention what the disobedient do in secret. But everything exposed by the light becomes visible, for it is light that makes everything visible. This is why it is said:
> "Wake up, O sleeper,
> rise from the dead,
> and Christ will shine on you."

What God wants us to understand is when we get close to a man by doing things with the guy you are interested in as if you were a married couple, we are out of His will. God wants us to share this depth of involvement with our husbands. If a man can't see you all the time and can't talk to you all the time, you aren't physically, emotionally, or spiritually one with him until he marries you, then there's a reason to get married—because he wants more. He wants the whole package because you haven't given him everything. Sometimes we give too much and do too much and wonder why a man doesn't marry us. Why should he marry us when he is getting everything he wants without the commitment?

A lady understands that criticizing, begging, nagging, controlling, and complaining only brings about disconnect in relationships. She realizes that a pattern of demanding and condemning behavior will destroy a relationship. She looks for ways to discuss differences without condemnation. She gives constructive suggestions without being demanding. She understands if she wants to see a different behavior in her man, she is to teach him a better way. Second Timothy 2:24 says, "And the Lord's servant must not quarrel; instead, he must be kind to everyone, able to teach, not resentful."

A lady doesn't allow herself to become just a piece of a man's equation. Often, men date multiple women. They get their sexual satisfaction from one woman. They get their financial needs taken care of by another woman. They like the way a third woman cooks. They like talking to that woman. They are getting their needs met by several different women, and they have no need to settle down with any of them. Why should they?

We have to be smart enough to not be one of the pieces—pieces of satisfaction. Lord, help us to disconnect from these pieces of relationships. If a man doesn't want all of us, he can't have part of us—a piece.

If you see yourself in this situation, just pull back. Put some space in the relationship. Put some distance and boundaries in place.

Most importantly, a lady knows to follow Proverbs 3:5–8 and trust in the Lord with all her heart and lean not on her own understanding; in all her ways acknowledge him, and he will direct her path. She is not wise in her own eyes; she fears the Lord and shuns evil, which will bring health to her body and nourishment to her bones.

# 17

## Solitude

Jesus calls us from loneliness to solitude. The fear of being left alone petrifies people. It drives us to noise and crowds. I remember getting my hysterectomy. My instructions from the doctor were to take it easy for two weeks, then based on my condition at that time, I could go back to work.

I was at home by myself for three days, and it almost drove me crazy. I packed my bags, got in my SUV, and headed for Atlanta from Dallas. I thought the twelve-hour drive was too much, so I drove to Memphis to visit a friend to break the drive up. I visited with her for the weekend, then drove the rest of the way to Atlanta. Two days before I was due back to work, I got up and made the twelve-hour drive back to Arlington. Thinking back on that time, I had to ask myself why couldn't I have stayed in my apartment in Arlington by myself for the two weeks.

The events that happened after my hysterectomy were the catalyst by which I was able to see and address my issues. "What was I afraid of?" was one question that came to mind. The other was, "Why would I date someone who disrespected me?"

The answer is quite simple. I was afraid of being alone.

Loneliness and chatter are not our only alternatives. We can cultivate an inner solitude and silence that sets us free from loneliness and fear. Loneliness is inner emptiness. Solitude is inner fulfillment.

Solitude is more a state of mind and heart than it is a place. There is a solitude of the heart that can be maintained at all times. Crowds—or the lack of them—have little to do with this inward peace. If we possess inward solitude, we do not fear being alone, for we know we are not alone. Neither do we fear being with others, for they do not control us. In the midst of noise and confusion, we are settled into a deep inner silence. God said He would never leave us or forsake us. You are never alone.

Inward solitude has outward manifestations. There is the freedom to be alone, not in order to be away from people but in order to hear the Divine Whisper better. Jesus frequently experienced solitude. He inaugurated His ministry by spending forty days alone in the desert. Matthew 4:1–2 says, "Then Jesus was led by the Spirit into the desert to be tempted by the devil. After fasting forty days and forty nights, he was hungry."

Before He chose the twelve disciples, He spent the entire night alone in the desert hills. Luke 6:12–13 says, "One of those days Jesus went out to a mountainside to pray, and spent the night praying to God. When morning came, he called his disciples to him and chose twelve of them, whom he also designated apostles."

Mark 1:35 says, "Very early in the morning, while it was still dark, Jesus got up, left the house and went off to a solitary place, where he prayed."

"The apostles gathered around Jesus and reported to him all they had done and taught. Then, because so many people were coming and going that they did not even have a chance to eat, he said to them, 'Come with me by yourselves to a quiet place and get some rest.' So they went away by themselves in a boat to a solitary place" (Mark 6:30–32).

There are more examples in the Bible, but perhaps this is sufficient to show the seeking out of solitary places was a regular practice for Jesus, and so it should be for us.

After I purposefully spent time by myself, I was able to hear the gentle whisper of God's voice and realize that He was with me. I was able to sit alone and be just fine. I could be surrounded by many people and still alone, not engaged with anyone, and the solitude no longer bothered me. I had no need to engage someone in conversation. I had no need to always be busy doing something. I was no longer afraid of being by myself. I could be at a restaurant by myself and be completely fine. I knew I was never alone. I had purposefully felt what it was like to be by myself, and it wasn't bad. I found peace and calm and quiet. I had faced my fear. To seek solitude and see that it is okay to be by yourself frees you from the fear of being alone. It allows you to welcome and celebrate your aloneness. It was liberating to be just fine when I was by myself or in a crowd.

I realized it was because I was afraid to be by myself that I kept going back to Charles. Being able to be without a man and be comfortable by myself was truly liberating.

# 18

## Peace

After a year of being abstinent, God said to me, "The peace I give you will be better than any 'piece' you have ever had." I understood when He whispered those words to me that day. His Word had told me to be celibate and not fornicate. I had done what He said. My life was full, I was happy with myself and where He had me in that season. I was finally at peace.

It was when I was going to FRY's Electronic Store to get my laptop, which I had taken in for repairs, that He whispered to me, "The peace I give you is better than any 'piece,' you have ever had." He was right. I was a living witness my life was better now that I was walking in obedience than anytime before. He was telling the truth all along. I just needed to take Him at His word and believe, and He made a believer out of me. It took faith. It took doing what He said to reap the benefit.

Even when I didn't understand how it was possible to be happy not having sex, the concept was so foreign, I walked by faith not by sight. I didn't know what the end was going to be, but I trusted Him. When we walk in obedience, the "peace" God gives us is better than any "piece" we could ever have.

# MY TESTIMONY

God knew I missed a man's touch. It's funny, but I became more aware of the touch of the water when I was taking a shower. It soothed my body and felt so good. I became aware of the wind brushing against my skin when I walked outside. It was like God was using these things to touch me and caress me. It was just what I needed. I experienced a heightened sense of awareness where even my food had more flavor. I was eating the same things, but I was able to enjoy the goodness in everything. I found pleasure in simple things.

I started to see how beautiful nature was. There was beauty all around me. The colors were amazing. I would spend time outside, admiring God's handiwork, and it put a smile on my face and in my heart. God was providing for me. He was giving me brand-new mercies every day. It was up to me to see them. Oh, the peace I felt. Oh, the joy in my heart. Oh, to know Him is to love Him.

I became aware of the little blessings in my life. There were people at work who were mean to me and because of the working conditions, they retired. I didn't have to work with them anymore. I took my little sister and her siblings and cousins to a church picnic. They put my name in a drawing, and I won a flat screen HDTV. I had prayed for Sundays off from work for years, and He blessed me with Sundays off.

God blessed me in other ways, too. I had always hated speaking in front of people. I would get so nervous doing the announcements at church that I felt my knees shake. Then one day, I was recognized as big sister of the year for Big Brothers Big Sisters of North Texas and was asked to give a speech at the volunteer appreciation dinner. About a thousand people attended. I prayed about what I should say and practiced my speech, and God blessed me to do so well that people went on and on about how my speech had inspired them. *Nobody but God!*

# PEACE

Then I was asked by the White House to give a speech on volunteering for its Helping America's Youth conference, and the First Lady Laura Bush was there. God proved to be faithful again.

I just saw the blessings He was providing every day, all day. He gave me happy feet. My cup runneth over. I could understand why King David danced before the Lord.

One day, He told me to get up and go and pray in every room in my two-bedroom apartment. He didn't say what to pray for or why. He's God. He didn't have to tell me why. I got up and went in every room, every closet, and said, "In Jesus' name. In Jesus' name." To this day, I don't know what that was about. I just know I had to be obedient. He had said so, and that was good enough for me.

God told me to write down what I was feeling, what I was learning, what I had been through. Writing it down was therapeutic for me. I was able to get what I had gone through off my chest. It was good to get it out. It was good to release it.

# 19

# Accepting Christ As Your Savior

Maybe you have read this book and have said to yourself, "I want what she has. I want to walk in the light and out of darkness. I want to know Christ on a deeper level. I want to grow. I am sick and tired of being sick and tired."

There *is* hope. There is a more excellent way. And that way is to God through His Son, Jesus Christ. Here's what you need to know about salvation:

THE PROBLEM: All men are sinners when measured against the standards of a Holy God. Romans 3:23 says, "For all have sinned and fall short of the glory of God."

THE PREDICAMENT: There is nothing a person can do to earn or merit forgiveness and a right standing before a Holy God. Romans 4:4–5 says, "Now when a man works, his wages are not credited to him as a gift, but as an obligation. However, to the man who does not work but trusts God who justifies the wicked, his faith is credited as righteousness."

THE PROVISION: God loves us so much that He provided Jesus Christ, His Son, to take our place on the cross and pay the penalty for our sins. God loves us in spite of all the mistakes we have made. Romans 5:8 tells us, "But God demonstrates his own love for us in this: While we were still sinners, Christ died for us."

THE PARDON: God, through grace, is freely giving eternal life to every person who receives forgiveness for their sins through Jesus Christ. Romans 6:23 says, "For the wages of sin is death, but the gift of God is eternal life in Christ Jesus our Lord."

THE PROCESS: People must turn to the risen Lord Jesus Christ in faith and trust Him alone, apart from any human merit, to deliver them from their sins and bring them into a relationship with God. Romans 10:9–10 says, "That if you confess with your mouth, 'Jesus is Lord,' and believe in your heart that God raised him from the dead, you will be saved. For it is with your heart that you believe and are justified, and it is with your mouth that you confess and are saved."

Ask God to come into your life and show you the truth.

# 20

## The Prodigal Daughter

I was finished with this book and had started on my second one. During my meditation, I thought of some hurtful things I had experienced while dating Charles. I asked God, "Why do those things still hurt me so? Why can't I get those things out of my mind? Why do they still affect me like they do?"

Some days, I would think of Charles, and they would be happy thoughts, and I would miss him. Other days, I felt like I hated his guts. I couldn't understand why my emotions ran the gamut. They were all over the place, so I asked God why. He said because I had not forgiven Charles.

I had been waiting on Charles to ask me to forgive him. I had been waiting for him to say he was sorry for the way he had treated me, but God said I needed to forgive him for his sake as well as for my own. Right then and there I prayed, *Charles, I forgive you in the name of Jesus. I forgive you for the hurt you caused. I forgive you for breaking my heart into pieces. I forgive you.* The tears ran down my face, and I felt instantly better. God is a good God, I am here to tell you.

Once I was visiting Houston for my birthday and to celebrate the New Year, and my friends and I were attending a class on being single. Well, someone stood up as we were talking about fornication and mentioned that she struggled with having sex. She stated she knew sex before she knew Christ. The young lady was being transparent. Her concern was real for a lot of us. Then one young lady went to the mic and gave these instructions for the group. She read First Thessalonians 4:3–8, but she made it personal—she took out the *you* and inserted *I*. That made all the difference. Here we go:

> It is God's will that *I* should be sanctified: that *I* should avoid sexual immorality; that *I* should learn to control *my* own body in a way that is holy and honorable, not in passionate lust like the heathen, who do not know God; and that in this matter *I* should not wrong *my* brother or take advantage of him. The Lord will punish *me* for all such sins, as *they* have already told *me* and warned *me*. For God did not call *me* to be impure, but to live a holy life. Therefore, if *I* reject this instruction *I* do not reject man but God, who gives *me* his Holy Spirit.

God has given us his Holy Spirit to help us when we are weak. We must call on Him at those times and ask Him to help us, and He will show up and show out. First Corinthians 10:13 says, "No temptation has seized you except what is common to man. And God is faithful; He will not let you be tempted beyond what you can bear. But when you are tempted, he will also provide a way out so that you can stand up under it." Second Corinthians 12:9 (KJV) says, "And he said unto me, My grace is sufficient for thee: for my strength is made perfect in weakness."

We are to lean and depend on God. We are supposed to do our part too. We can stop looking at those sexually orientated TV programs. We can change what we listen to. We can surround ourselves with like-minded friends. Most of all, when we are having a moment, we can tell God all about it. He didn't say we wouldn't have our trials. He said He would help us through them. He doesn't take away your hotness. He gives you His Holy Spirit to assist you with your passion.

In January 2008, I received a text message from one of my friends saying Charles had asked her out. She wanted to know if I had a problem with her going. The text went like this:

Martha: HI, CHARLES ASKED ME 2 THE MOVIES, BUT I WON'T GO IF U HAVE A PROBLEM WITH IT.
Me: GIRL, GO. CHARLES IS A WONDERFUL GUY, AND YOU ARE A WONDERFUL PERSON!!!
BUT THANK YOU, SISTER, FOR CONSIDERING MY FEELINGS. THAT'S THE KIND OF SWEETHEART YOU ARE.
Martha: THAT'S SWEET, BUT I WOULDN'T GO IF U HAVE A PROBLEM WITH IT.
Me: BELIEVE ME, I DON'T.

Now when I first got the text, it threw me for a loop for about three seconds. But God had already fixed it in my spirit. He had shown me that it was okay to want what was best for Charles and look out for his best interests, even if it wasn't a relationship with me. God had shown me that a man will flaunt a woman in my face to make me jealous. I think Charles still has feelings for me and that he is going through all this effort to get my attention. He has done things like this in the past.

Let me start off by saying I had used these same tactics myself, which is why I recognized them when I saw them in Charles. Once I told a coworker I was engaged, hoping it would get back to Charles and make him jealous. Kirk had talked about us getting married, but in no way were we engaged.

What Charles had done was he and a guy friend had gone on a double date together and they had taken a girl named Nicole, who worked with us and who was infatuated with Charles, as a fifth wheel. After the date, what was the first thing she did? She ran back and told about it. She couldn't wait to get to work to tell me and my girlfriend how my ex was dating someone new. She couldn't stand me because she thought I had stolen him away from her. I can't help that he chose me.

Now why would he and his friend be on a double date and invite a single female along for the ride? And why would this female be someone who worked with both of us? He knew she would run back and tell it. He played her like a violin, and she didn't even realize he was using her. But I saw right through what he was doing.

Martha, who Charles asked to take to the movies, told me a week earlier he had called her and told her I wouldn't speak to him half the time. Now he wanted to take her on a date to the movies. How predictable can one man be? But I love it. It just shows me the kind of effort he will go through to get my attention.

Through all of this, I remembered God's promise: What God has for me is for me! My inheritance comes from the Father. And I was instantly okay with this situation. That is the peace that transcends all understanding that Paul talks about in Philippians 4:7.

We must always remember what God has told us which helps us work through our circumstances. We are to keep our eyes on Him and not what is going on, because God's got us.

I felt jealousy with the new girl when she arrived. But I had worked through that. Then when I saw Charles with my coworker, I didn't deny my feelings, but I worked through them by asking God why I felt that way. After God worked in me, I was ready when I got Martha's text. It's amazing how He prepares us for life and what's to come. That is what He was doing. He was preparing me. I had relied on Him in past situations. And He had prepared me to handle this situation. What a loving Father.

My destiny is ahead of me. I can choose to move backward, I can choose to remain here, or I can choose to move forward. I choose to move forward.

I had gone over a girlfriend's house for dinner. We talked about our present and past relationships. She thought I should make a move on Charles. See, that's exactly what he is counting on. He had asked my girlfriend out on a date so I would make a move toward him, step up my game because of the competition. It's not going to happen!

She thought since we still did things to incite and stir up each other that we should give it another chance. She has been in an on-again, off-again relationship for the past sixteen years. She was still talking to her ex-husband, who was re-married, and their kids were grown. I listened to what she was saying, and thought I didn't want to be in her shoes—not able to let go of the past and move forward. I want to cut that relationship off and be able to give myself fully to the man in my future. I want to release the old to make room for the new. I feel she won't be able to commit to someone new because she hasn't let go of her past. I don't want that to be me.

God can't bless her with what He has for her because she doesn't trust Him to provide. So what she is saying with her actions is she would rather keep seeing her ex because she thinks it's better to have something than nothing. It's fear. I choose to trust God. I let go and let God. I know He is able and will provide. That's what He loves to do.

Charles had broken up with me twice during our relationship. God gave me a revelation about why Charles had broken up with me. He said Charles wanted me to get to the place where I was crying after him, "Don't leave me, don't leave me," when he broke up with me those two times. He wanted to see me fall out over him and run and chase behind him. I said my peace and was gone. As women, we must read between the lines and see what the men in our lives are trying to do to us. See their motives.

# In Conclusion

I heard a sermon titled, "I'm In It To Win It." There were several points that the pastor made:

When you are making positive changes in your life, there will always be those around you who want to get in your way—the sharks. Life can be cold and cloudy but don't give up because you can't see your way where you desire to go. You've got to be in it to win it.

The second point was that we must live a life of excellence. We must make up our minds to define ourselves. You decide who you are. How you date is a reflection of how you see yourself. Take notice. Then when you decide who you are, no one else can tell you who you are.

There is power in identity. We must stop allowing others and circumstances to define us.

Next, visualize the prize that orders your steps. Decide on your purpose and where you are going, then decide on who is going on the journey with you. Some people will be discarded. Some stuff is weighing you down and holding you back. You can't be with someone who is going down when you want to go up.

After this sermon, my mind was clear that Charles was not the one for me. I still loved him, but I knew that the journey God has for my life would be with someone just as passionate as I am for the kingdom, hence all of the missed opportunities for us to get together. In each one, God was trying to tell me something and that something was "No, not this one."

So I moved on, realizing the best is yet to come.

After being in difficult and hurtful relationships, I know your present season can be a difficult one for you. Just take it one step at a time. Trust me—it *will* get better. I felt overwhelmed with it all at first. But each day, I would talk to God more and more about the way I felt or what was bothering me. I would ask Him why, and I would ask Him to help me. I ran to whichever church was having a singles event so I could learn more of God's ways. I joined different Bible studies so I could learn, and I decided I would dedicate my body to the Father and sacrifice not having sex. I decided I wanted to live a holy, righteous, and a sanctified life. I would pursue a relationship with Jesus and be desperate for Him instead of a man or anything else. This relationship changed my life. I was finally at peace. I had direction. I had a purpose. I had confidence and assurance. I had love.

Because my mental condition had improved, I noticed my physical ailments also improved. I was a new creature. Jesus wants us to be clean and whole, and He will make us whole if we would just ask and believe. I had restless leg syndrome. After reading so many times in the Bible Jesus saying your faith has made you whole. I said, "Lord, I'm your child and you love me. I know you want me whole and not inflicted with this disease, and I hate taking these pills. I know you can heal me. I believe you will."

That day I threw away my bottle of pills. I have been healed ever since. Just say as the man with leprosy said, "Lord, if you are willing, you can make me clean." He is willing. He just wants you to ask Him. You are not in this by yourself.

God is bigger than your problem. God is bigger than your pain. He wants to help you and make you whole. Just ask Him to.

*To God be the glory for all the things He has done, is doing, and will do.*

# Notes

Deepak Chopra. *The Seven Spiritual Laws of Success* © 1994. Reprinted by permission of Amber-Allen Publishing, Inc., P. O. Box 6657, San Rafael, CA 94903. All rights reserved.

Richard J. Foster. *Celebration of Discipline: The Path to Spiritual Growth.* New York: HarperCollins Publisher, 1998.

Ken Sande. *The Peacemaker: A Biblical Guide to Resolving Personal Conflict.* Grand Rapids, MI: Baker Books, 2004.

Richard Warren. *The Purpose-Driven Life: What on Earth Am I Here For?* Grand Rapids, MI: Zondervan, 2002.

Dr. Henry Cloud and Dr. John Townsend. *Participant's Guide, Making Dating Work: Boundaries in Dating.* Grand Rapids, MI: Zondervan, 2000.

Dr. Henry Cloud and Dr. John Townsend. *Boundaries: When to Say YES When to Say NO To Take Control of Your Life.* Grand Rapids, MI: Zondervan, 1992.

Cynthia Heald. *Maybe God is Right After All: And Other Radical Ideas to Live By.* Carol Stream, Illinois: Tyndale House, 2005.

Kay Arthur. *LORD, Where Are You When Bad Things Happen?*

Colorado Springs, Colorado: Waterbrook Press, 1992.

Ellen Fein and Sherrie Schneider. *The Rules: Time-tested Secrets for Capturing the Heart of Mr. Right.* New York, NY: Warner Books, Inc., 1995.